In *Simulating sovereignty* Cynthia Weber presents a critical analysis of the concept of sovereignty. Examining the justifications for intervention offered by the Concert of Europe, President Wilson's Administration, and the Reagan–Bush Administrations, she combines critical international relations theory and foreign policy discourses about intervention to accomplish two important goals. First, rather than redefining state sovereignty, she radically deconstructs it by questioning the historical foundations of sovereign authority. Secondly, the book provides a critique of representation generally, and of the representation of the sovereign state in particular. This book is thus an original and important contribution to the understanding of sovereignty, the state and intervention in international relations theory.

D1560376

SIMULATING SOVEREIGNTY

Cambridge Studies in International Relations is a joint initiative of Cambridge University Press and the British International Studies Association (BISA). The series will include a wide range of material, from undergraduate textbooks and surveys to research-based monographs and collaborative volumes. The aim of the series is to publish the best new scholarship in International Studies from Europe, North America and the rest of the world.

CAMBRIDGE STUDIES IN INTERNATIONAL RELATIONS

Series list continues after index

SIMULATING SOVEREIGNTY:
INTERVENTION, THE STATE, AND SYMBOLIC EXCHANGE

CYNTHIA WEBER

Purdue University

CAMBRIDGE
UNIVERSITY PRESS

Published by the Press Syndicate of the University of Cambridge
The Pitt Building, Trumpington Street, Cambridge CB2 1RP
40 West 20th Street, New York, NY 10011–4211, USA
10 Stamford Road, Oakleigh, Melbourne 3166, Australia

© Cambridge University Press 1995

First published 1995

Printed in Great Britain at the University Press, Cambridge

A catalogue record for this book is available from the British Library

Library of Congress cataloguing in publication data

Weber, Cynthia.
Simulating sovereignty: intervention, the state and symbolic
exchange / Cynthia Weber.
        p.   cm. – (Cambridge studies in international relations: 37)
ISBN 0 521 45523 5
1. Sovereigny.   2. Intervention (International law)
3. International relations.   I. Title.   II. Series.
JC327.W45   1995
320.1'5 – dc20   94-9269   CIP

ISBN 0521 45523 5 hardback
ISBN 0521 45559 6 paperback

For Summa

CONTENTS

PREFACE

Sovereignty is often treated by international relations theorists as a foundational concept. Investigations of the state more and more frequently critically analyze the foundational status of sovereignty. Such analyses require more than just making the claim that sovereignty is a variable concept. They entail shifting through the various ways in which this seemingly foundational concept has been reconfigured in diplomatic practice. To do this effectively, the concept of sovereignty ought not to be examined in isolation either from history or from related theoretical terms. Additionally, attention must be directed to the ways in which various meanings of sovereignty, as they shift and are reformed, have been configured.

I investigate the relationship between sovereignty and its supposed conceptual opposite – intervention – because, as I argue, the sovereignty/intervention boundary is the very location of the state. I present a number of theoretical arguments to support this assertion. Then I turn to historical analyses of intervention practices by the Concert of Europe, the Wilson administration, and the Reagan–Bush administrations in which I trace the constitution and interpretation of community standards for legitimate intervention practices and their corresponding effects upon collective understandings of state sovereignty.

I weave critical international relations theory (informed by the works of Michel Foucault and Jean Baudrillard) into foreign policy discourses of intervention to accomplish two theoretical tasks. First, rather than redefining state sovereignty, this analysis "un"-defines (and therefore radically deconstructs) state sovereignty by questioning the historical foundations of sovereign authority. Secondly, this analysis provides a critique of representation generally and of the representation of the sovereign state in particular.

I suggest that the meanings of sovereignty no longer abide by what I term a logic of representation (in which referents [signifeds] and indicators [signifiers] are clearly demarcated) but instead abide by a logic of simulation (in which there are no ultimate foundations but instead a chain of interchangeable signifiers). Theorizing the relationship between state sovereignty and intervention in a logic of simulation (and in a system of symbolic exchange) requires that we cease to assume representational relationships and pose representation as a question. Instead of asking "what is represented?" or "what are represented as the foundations of state sovereignty?" we now ask "how does the representation assumption affect our understandings of state sovereignty and intervention?" For international relations theorists to contribute to understandings of sovereignty, the state, and intervention, the failure of representation must be acknowledged and serious consideration must be given to the simulation of sovereignty. I begin this project here by examining how sovereignty might be simulated in contemporary diplomatic practice and how simulation transforms international relations theories of state sovereignty and intervention.

ACKNOWLEDGMENTS

This book has been a long time in the making. Along the way, innumerable people have taught me and encouraged me. Richard Ashley, Patrick McGowan, and Stephen Walker have been involved with this project from the beginning. I owe them my greatest intellectual debts. I was fortunate to spend a year at the Center for International Studies at the University of Southern California working on the early research and writing of this book. There, I benefited from conversations with Ian Bell, Thomas Biersteker, John Odell, and Jim Rosenau, among others. Another person I met at USC was Carolyn King who rescued me from my limited French by translating diplomatic correspondences into English.

Over the years, Roxanne Doty, Marianne Marchand, and Eric Selbin have engaged me in lively debates about sovereignty and poststructuralism. Surely, they have saved me from many a misstep. At critical moments, David Campbell, James Der Derian, Lisa Freeman, Richard Little, Tim Luke, Michael Shapiro, John Vasquez, and Rob Walker offered sage advice on how to present my arguments. Students, staff, and faculty at Purdue University provided me with encouragement and support, particularly Diane Rubenstein who read almost as many drafts of the emerging text as did I. Like Diane, Michael Weinstein kept me theoretically honest. Also, Carol Pech provided editorial and research assistance, as did Francois Debrix. I thank them all.

Finally, without the support of my friends in West Virginia, I may have done something "pragmatic" like get a law degree. I thank them for tolerating my impracticalities and for helping me to place my academic endeavors in perspective. This book is dedicated to my grandmother Hilda Lilyan Fyfe, who offered me similar combinations of unconditional personal support and cheerful intellectual disinterest.

Research support for this book has been provided by the Center for International Studies at the University of Southern California where I was a visiting scholar in 1989–90 and by the Purdue University

Research Foundation in the form of a summer research grant and an international travel grant.

Parts of this work have appeared elsewhere. Parts of chapters 1 and 5 appeared in *Alternatives* (Summer 1992) under the title "Writing Sovereign Identities: Wilson Administration Intervention in the Mexican Revolution." An earlier draft of chapter 2 appeared in *Review of International Studies* (July 1992) as "Reconsidering Statehood: Examining the Sovereignty/Intervention Boundary." I thank the editors of these journals and their publishers for allowing these articles to be incorporated into this book.

Finally, I wish to thank Steve Smith and Michael Holdsworth of Cambridge University Press for recruiting this book to be in the Cambridge International Studies Series.

1 WRITING THE STATE

Can one say anything about statehood without beginning by deciding what sovereignty means? When this question is considered in light of most of the literature in international relations, the answer appears to be probably not. Few scholars would admit this answer, yet when one considers how international relations theorists give accounts of history, concepts, and issues in their discipline, they seemingly are presented with a choice between two opposed options. They may provide explanations from within the tradition of realism which takes individual sovereign states as its point of departure. Alternatively, they may give their accounts from within the tradition of idealism which takes a community of sovereign states as its point of departure.[1] Either way, sovereignty is a central component of their discussions. Sovereignty describes states either individually or in a community. Thus sovereignty serves as a fundamental point of reference in international relations, a ground or essential modifier for the state.

Even though the concept of sovereignty performs as a referent for statehood, debates in the international relations literature suggest that the meaning of sovereignty is not clearly defined (Biersteker et al., 1993). Generally, sovereignty is taken to mean the absolute authority a state holds over a territory and people as well as independence internationally and recognition by other sovereign states as a sovereign state. However, when confronted by questions about the specific meaning of sovereignty, international relations theorists readily admit that precisely what sovereignty means remains rather fuzzy. In response to this problem of meaning, theorists may follow Ernst Haas who once wrote, "I do not use the concept at all and see no need to" (1969:70), thereby neglecting the concept altogether. Recently, however, a more common response by theorists has been to make sovereignty the focus of their work, examining more how the concept functions in international relations than precisely what sovereignty means.[2] Acknowledging the ambiguity of the meaning of state sovereignty, theorists defer questions of meaning in favor of pressing on to

1

investigate "serious" questions of international relations, all the while referring back to the sovereign state. In effect, then, theorists "solve" (however temporarily) the problem of state sovereignty by proceeding as if the meaning of sovereignty were stable because a solution to this problem seems to be a prerequisite for getting on with the business of international relations theory. With this in mind, R.B.J. Walker noted that far from its largely accepted status as an "essentially contested" concept,[3] state sovereignty is instead an essentially *un*contested concept. Walker writes of sovereign statehood:

> Its meaning might be marginally contestable by constitutional lawyers and other connoisseurs of fine lines, but for the most part state sovereignty expresses a commanding silence. At least some problems of political life, it seems to suggest, are simple and settled, fit for legalists and footnotes, but not of pressing concern to those interested in the cut and thrust of everyday political struggle.
>
> (Walker, 1990:1)

Treating state sovereignty as an already settled question leads to two embarrassments for international relations theorists. The first is a blindness to the historicity of sovereignty. Not one but countless forms of state sovereignty co-exist in modern global political life. For example, sovereignty refers to democratic, authoritarian, and totalitarian regimes, to socialist and capitalist domestic political/economic systems, and to First, Second, Third and now Fourth and Fifth World governments. What international relations theorists must not see is that what counts and/or functions as sovereign is not the same in all times and places.[4]

Adding to this confusion is the observation that the range of state power – what a state can do, what its competencies are and what the limits to its powers are with respect to society and humanity, for example – has profoundly changed historically. Not only do various forms of sovereign statehood co-exist in distinct locales in modern global politics, but added to this spatial dimension of sovereignty[5] is a temporal variation as well. The legitimate privileges and competencies of states are markedly different in the eighteenth, nineteenth, and twentieth centuries.[6]

These spatial and temporal dimensions of sovereignty, account in part for how competing descriptions claiming to capture the essential nature of sovereignty and thus statehood can co-exist in modern global political discourse. They do so by taking a particular historically and spatially specific example as their empirical referent (for example, post-World War II Western industrial nation-states) and universalizing this form of sovereignty to the entire history of sovereignty (or to

2

the entire history of authority relations more generally)[7] in every locale.

Taking these observations about sovereignty seriously, some scholars suggest that while the word sovereignty denotes a state of being – an ontological status – sovereignty in fact expresses a characteristic way in which being or sovereign statehood may be inferred from doing or practice. It is not possible to talk about the state as an ontological being – as a political identity – without engaging in the political practice of constituting the state. Put differently, to speak of the sovereign state at all requires one to engage in the political practice of stabilizing this concept's meaning. Thought of in this way, sovereignty marks not the location of the foundational entity of international relations theory but a site of political struggle. This struggle is the struggle to fix the meaning of sovereignty in such a way as to constitute a particular state – to write the state – with particular boundaries, competencies and legitimacies available to it. This is not a one-time occurrence which fixes the meaning of sovereignty and statehood for all time in all places; rather, this struggle is repeated in various forms at numerous spatial and temporal locales.

The second embarrassment for international relations theorists who presume settlement of the question of sovereignty, then, is that they cannot begin to investigate how the meaning of sovereignty is stabilized. They must close their eyes to what is without a doubt the most fundamental of political questions – how is the meaning of state sovereignty fixed in theory and practice?

It is just this question that is the focus of this study. What is *not* attempted here is to trace historically how sovereignty has been defined by theorists or legal scholars (to provide a genealogy of sovereignty) and then to choose which definition is best or most useful. Nor does this study attempt to refine vague definitions of sovereignty and offer my own more precise, exact understanding of the concept so a better understanding of statehood can be achieved. Instead, this study investigates another question: How is the meaning of sovereignty fixed or stabilized historically via practices of international relations theorists and practices of political intervention? In other words, how do practices of theorists and diplomats stabilize the meaning of sovereignty and, by default, write the state?

These introductory remarks have suggested that practices by international relations theorists participate in the stabilization of the meaning of state sovereignty. How intervention practices fit into this analysis has yet to be elaborated. In contrast to existing studies of intervention, this investigation does not begin by defining interven-

3

tion as a violation of state sovereignty and proceeding to classify cases with reference to this rule. Rather, intervention practices are examined because they raise the very question of sovereignty.

Intervention practices participate in stabilizing the meaning of sovereignty. This is so because discussions of intervention invariably imply questions of sovereignty. In modern global political discourse, intervention generally infers a violation of state sovereignty (Vincent, 1974; Little, 1975; Bull, 1984). Thus, intervention discourse begins by positing a sovereign state with boundaries that might be violated and then regards transgressions of these boundaries as a problem. Furthermore, intervention practices take analysis immediately to the question of when, from a reputedly global perspective, sovereignty is or is not invested in a particular locality, leadership, or set of practices. When state practices do not fit intersubjective understandings of what a sovereign state must be, then interference by a sovereign state into the affairs of an "aberrant" state is legitimate. Moreover, such practices rarely are referred to as interventions. On the other hand, when state practices do accord with intersubjective understandings of being or statehood, intervention is prohibited and, when carried out, condemned by the supposed community of sovereign states.[8] By focusing on intervention practices, it is possible to identify examples of what forms of doing – state practices – constitute legitimate forms of being – sovereign states. By analyzing interventions which occurred at different historical periods, it is possible to get indications of how intervention justifications, sovereignty and statehood have changed.[9]

Two additional aspects of how the question of sovereignty arises in intervention practices bear mention. Both have to do with the constitution of communities – communities of sovereign states, on the one hand, and communities as the foundations for sovereign states, on the other. To begin with how the constitution of communities of sovereign states is raised by intervention practices, it would be beneficial to illustrate this point with reference to a popular theme in international relations research in the 1980s and 1990s – norms. In a situation of structural anarchy, neorealist theorists ask, how can norms be explained? Prevailing wisdom holds that norms are the result of interest coordination and often are expressed as regimes – informal institutions around which interests converge (Krasner, 1983).

For the concept of norms to be meaningful in global political life, there must exist an interpretive community to evaluate state practices in the light of prevailing norms. These issue-specific interpretive communities often are expressed as the origins of norms rather than as

4

their effects. That is, according to this logic, state practices encounter interpretive standards that are always already in place before practices occur, and these standards emanate from an already existing interpretive community. Interpretive communities appear to exist prior to state practices because in giving an explanation for the existence of norms, neorealist theorists must assume both sovereign states and interpretive communities *a priori*. Very few theorists question this logic, much less turn it around by asking how interpretive communities can be said to exist before interests converge.[10]

Intervention practices raise the question of the constitution of a community of sovereign states in a similar way. When intervention practices occur, they are accompanied by justifications on the part of an intervening state to a supposed international community of sovereign states. In offering justifications for their intervention practices, diplomats of intervening states simultaneously assume the existence of norms regulating state practices and an interpretive community that will judge intervention practices in accordance with these norms. But just as in the case of international regimes, it is international practice that constitutes the boundaries and capacities of both sovereign states and international interpretive communities. Rather than diplomats addressing their justifications for intervention to an already formed community, the form of a justification in effect participates in the constitution of both the state as a sovereign identity and the interpretive community to which the state's justifications are directed.

I do not mean to suggest that when undertaking an act of intervention and offering an apology for this act, spokespersons for a sovereign state consciously configure their audience into a community of similarly disposed sovereign states. On the contrary, implicit in a state's offering of a justification for its practices is the assumption that a community of sovereign states which abides by similar norms of conduct *already* exists.

The question of community constitution also arises with reference to the constitution of the sovereign voice of a state. Implicit in the notion that diplomats offer justifications to interpretive communities[11] is the assumption that the state for whom the diplomat speaks is also already fully constituted as a sovereign identity. That is, the state has the capacity to speak on behalf of its domestic constituency on matters of global politics and deserves to be heard.[12] Such an assumption neglects a number of questions pertaining to the constitution of the state as a sovereign identity.

For a state to have a voice in global politics, it must speak for its domestic constituency, and this constituency must already be

5

organized into a community. But how can this community be said to exist, and how can the state be said to speak on its behalf? It seems that a number of things are required. Primarily, a domestic community must be differentiated from both the realm of global politics and from other domestic communities. This is no easy matter considering that the boundaries marking off a domestic community are not naturally given, uncontested, and fixed. Boundaries are transgressed by both domestic groups excluded by the state (the disenfranchised, be they minorities, homeless or criminals, for example) as well as external groups (such as refugees and illegal aliens). If one includes in the notion of boundaries not just physical phenomena like peoples and geography but also less tangible phenomena like authority, it becomes quite difficult to locate anything resembling a stable boundary. One need only think of the permeability of state authority in economics – expressed in terms like "interdependence" (Keohane and Nye, 1977) and "sovereignty at bay" (Vernon, 1971 and 1991) – security – aired in debates about "the demise of the territorial state" due to the existence of nuclear weapons (Herz, 1957)[13] – or ecology – highlighted by noting that such things as acid rain, pollution, and the disposal of nuclear waste defy territorial boundaries (Walker, 1988).[14] Taken together, these transgressions make it difficult to imagine not only boundaries but also "domestic" as opposed to "international" spaces not to mention "communities." They shift the focus of analysis away from questions such as "who is and is not a member of a particular domestic community?" to questions such as "how is it possible to speak of 'communities' at all?"

Positing a state with a sovereign voice in global politics disallows these kinds of questions because any such positing presupposes the existence of a domestic community. Yet even if theorists assume the existence of a domestic community, they still confront another question: how does this community serve as the voice of sovereign authority for the state? This is very much tied to the notion of the way in which practice or "doing" implies ontology or "being." For a state to be sovereign, it must represent its domestic community in global politics. Representation is meant in two senses. The first meaning of representation might be called "political representation" which refers to an exchange that is supposed to occur between the state and its domestic community. The notion here is that a domestic community authorizes the formal apparatus of the state – the government – to speak on its behalf in both domestic and global politics.[15]

Political representation presupposes another aspect of representation, what might be termed "symbolic representation." Symbolic representation concerns the logic of representational projects and the strategies by which they are pursued. According to a logic of representation, language is always tied to some empirical referent, foundation, or ground that is always the basis for speech. Expressed in terms of semiotics or sign theory, a signifier (indicator) always refers back to a signified (referent which is represented by the indicator). And even though, as Saussure argued, this relationship between the signifier and signified is a cultural and not natural phenomena, the relationship between a signifier and a signified remains within a logic of representation so long as it is held that a signifier must refer back to a signified (Saussure, 1974).

Thinking through the problem of the transference of authority from a domestic community to a state government within a logic of representation and semiotics, one might suggest that a domestic community is the signified to which a state government or signifier refers when pointing to the source of its sovereign authority. But, as suggested earlier, the boundaries of a domestic community are in flux. Questions not only of who is and is not a member of a domestic community but also what the range of authority of a domestic community might be are unsettled in practice. For a logic of representation to work – for a domestic community to serve as the signified or point of reference – these and similar questions about the boundaries of a domestic community must be resolved.

A logic of representation necessarily excludes these types of questions. For how can one preserve the notion of representation – that a signifier refers back to a signified – if either no signified or ground can be said to exist or if a signified or ground is constituted in the act of speech? Put differently, how can one say that a transference of authority somehow takes place between a domestic community and its government apparatus if either there is no stable domestic community or if a domestic community is constituted or made up to serve as the foundation of sovereign authority within a state in the very act of speaking about this domestic community?

For a logic of representation to work, a signified or ground must exist. And if no signified or ground can be found, one must be created. Thus, in the case of the transference of authority from a domestic community to a state government, symbolic representation begins by taking that which does not exist except as a fiction – a domestic community – and transforming it into the foundation of the sovereign authority of the state. Working within the logic of representation and asking "who is the sovereign authority in a domestic community which is represented by a state?" an answer must be "found" or

7

"produced" or the logic of representation will crumble. For a logic of representation to be politically effective, this question must be postponed. It must not be asked, for the mere asking of questions about foundational authorities puts foundational authorities into question. "Finding" answers concerning who foundational authorities are may not be enough to make a logic of representation work; a more successful strategy is to prevent such questions from ever being raised.[16]

Historically, who has served as the sovereign authority within domestic communities or, to put the issue somewhat differently, where sovereignty has resided, has changed. Until the late 1700s, sovereignty was said to reside in the political body of the monarch. But the sovereign figure Bodin described in his *Six Livres de la Republique* in 1576 as providential investment in a ruler who is to be a mortal god is no longer the foundational authority of modern states. Beginning in the seventeenth century, emerging in the struggles of the eighteenth century, and taking practical political form in the early nineteenth century, sovereignty has been expressed as the popular mode whereby a citizenry represents itself and submits itself to the authority of the state so long as the state performs as the reflection of the will of its citizenry.[17] Monarchical sovereignty has given way to popular sovereignty, and popular sovereignty has come to be understood in terms of representation – both political and symbolic. Increasingly, both the political and symbolic representation of "the people" has become difficult, to the point where the feasibility of representational logics has become a question (Baudrillard, 1988). Yet because the sovereign voice of a supposed domestic community is assumed when theorists refer to sovereign states, questions concerning how one form of sovereignty came to replace another and whether theories should continue to be expressed in representational terms cannot be raised by international relations theorists.

These observations about the constitution of communities in theoretical discourses about state sovereignty underscore how theorists as well as diplomats "solve" the problem of community constitution by positing *a priori* the existence of sovereign states so that questions of community constitution are not asked. But in diplomatic practice, bringing closure to these issues is not as simple, particularly in the face of intervention practices. This is because intervention is a moment of modern global political life during which legal, formalized boundaries become politically contested and communities as points of reference – be they "domestic" foundations of state sovereignty or "international" centers of judgment – are brought into doubt. That the formalization and legitimation of boundaries are the effects of coordinated inter-

8

national practices is most evident when – as in the case of intervention – coordinated practices break down. Diplomatic practice, much like international relations theory, assumes boundaries as accomplished facts of global political life. As in international relations theory, diplomatic practice assumes that global political practices are not imposed by some supra-national coordinator. Rather, what coordination occurs among practices is worked out in practice and, therefore, is the effect of practice. This study begins to tell the story of how these collaborations are effected by focusing on intervention practices.

Telling this story involves making three refusals. First, one must refuse to "solve" the question of sovereign statehood and instead pose sovereignty as a question. Doing so requires putting both sovereignty and statehood in doubt or under erasure.[18] Not only must boundaries, competencies, and legitimacies of states be regarded as permeable, mobile effects of practice and sovereignty as an ideal descriptive of modern political authority relations that most probably will never take practical political form, but also a skepticism must be brought to the possibility of speaking of sovereignty and statehood without imposing an answer onto the question of state sovereignty. To avoid replicating this act of closure so common to international relations theory, no definition of sovereignty is offered. Rather, definitions produced under specific historical circumstances – particularly at moments of intervention practices – will be analyzed not by asking if they capture the "real," "true" meaning of sovereignty but by focusing on how these historically specific meanings affect forms of being or states.

Secondly, one must refuse to position oneself outside of history with respect to questions of sovereign statehood and intervention. International relations theorists regularly claim to occupy positions outside of history. These scholars, whether studying sovereign statehood or intervention, begin by positing sovereignty as a "first" (Vincent, 1974) or "constitutive" (Ruggie, 1983; Wendt, 1988)[19] principle that is the defining characteristic of the modern state system. In so doing, they demarcate the modern state system from previous forms of political organization and, owing a debt to this first act of differentiation, go on to explain subsequent practices of inclusion and exclusion. Such a position not only reproduces the practices of inclusion and exclusion that are very much bound up in questions of sovereignty but also casts a blind eye toward anything which eludes or defies this sovereign gaze back on history (Walker, 1993).

One such casualty of this position is the question of change. While some explanation for the origins of the modern state system are generally given by these theorists, no account of changes within the

9

system can be forwarded. For example, consider John Ruggie's work. Ruggie explains the emergence of the modern state system with reference to the emergence of private property. However, if one hopes to analyze the shifting basis of sovereign authority expressed by the displacement of monarchical sovereignty by popular sovereignty, one cannot do so within Ruggie's framework. This is so because for Ruggie history is the history of continuities within the modern state system, and sovereignty is that which grounds these continuities.[20] If we are to posit sovereignty as a constitutive principle, we confront once again the concern of bringing closure to questions of sovereignty from the outset of analysis.

Thirdly, one must refuse to affirm a logic of representation as a regulative ideal of discourse. This refusal acknowledges that representational projects and the strategies by which they are effected depend upon the creative deployment of symbolic resources that are not inexhaustible. With respect to sovereign statehood, then, we may be reaching an exacting point when enactments of sovereign statehood in practice are depleting their own resources to the point where there is little room for creative redeployment of these resources.

As a result, sovereignty as a practice may not be able to be replicated in modern global political life forever. Intervention practices carried out today – for example the US occupation of the sovereign state of Panama and capture of Panamanian Head of State General Manuel Noriega in December 1989 – raise the question "what, if anything, does sovereignty mean in the contemporary world?" In the face of such practices, it is misguided to retreat to an international legal definition of sovereignty as (among other things) a state's absolute authority over its domestic affairs.[21] Furthermore, it is fruitless to attempt to locate a domestic community that can be said to be the sovereign authority in a state. Might it be that sovereignty has no foundation? Might analyses of sovereignty benefit from a break from the logic of representation and a consideration of sovereign practices as self-referential, organized according to a post-representational logic of simulation? Put differently, it is no longer sufficient to ask "how is sovereignty represented?" International relations scholars must move on to another question, "how is sovereignty simulated?"

2 EXAMINING THE SOVEREIGNTY/INTERVENTION BOUNDARY

What R.B.J. Walker wrote about the uncontested meaning of sovereignty applies equally to the intervention literature. Intervention is an essentially *un*contested concept. The uncontestedness of intervention has to do with its coupling with sovereignty. This coupling of sovereignty and its transgressor continues to define the gambit of imaginable research programs for intervention scholars. It is not the mere linking of the concepts sovereignty and intervention that presents an obstacle to offering unique contributions about intervention. Rather, similar to Walker's remarks on the sovereignty debates, I argue that the particular understandings of sovereignty/intervention circulating in international relations literatures effect a silence. This silence is on potentially dynamic understandings of statehood. As Richard Little concluded in his review of the intervention literature, "For specialists in international relations to contribute to this debate about intervention, they will require a much more sophisticated conception of the state than the one usually relied upon" (Little, 1987:54). I suggest that understandings of sovereignty/intervention currently employed by international relations theorists inhibit creative reconceptualizations of statehood. Yet if we as theorists think about sovereign statehood in terms of authority relations which are worked out in practice and that the sovereignty/intervention boundary is an important locale where authority relations are contested, then examining the intersections of discourses of sovereignty and intervention takes us a long way toward giving an account of how sovereign states are constituted in practice.[1] Accordingly, my analytical point of departure for a "more sophisticated conception of the state" is a re-examination of the sovereignty/intervention boundary.[2]

Such a positioning implies a break from the well-rehearsed practice of defining intervention as a violation of state sovereignty and proceeding to categorize specific episodes of historical practices as interventionary or noninterventionary. It further implies a refusal to stabilize the meanings of sovereignty and intervention through some

11

grand theoretical gesture which enables such classification exercises. Finally, it implies a recognition that the meanings of sovereignty and intervention are inscribed, contested, erased, and reinscribed through historical practices. Focusing on the interplay of the meanings of sovereignty and intervention, this chapter suggests that modalities of sovereign statehood are effects of the contestation of meanings of both sovereignty and intervention. Furthermore, the arenas where meanings of sovereignty/intervention are contested include practices both by diplomats and by international relations theorists. Each of these is analyzed in turn.

Diplomatic Practices and Intervention

Consider the following historical episodes. Austrian Chancellor Metternich remarking on behalf of the Concert of Europe about revolutions in Spain and Naples in the 1820s wrote:

> States belonging to the European alliance, which have undergone in their internal structure an alternation brought about by revolt, whose consequences may be dangerous to other states, cease automatically to be members of the alliance. [If such states] cause neighboring states to feel an immediate danger, and if action by the Great Powers can be effective and beneficial, the Great Powers will take steps to bring the disturbed area back into the European system, first of all by friendly representations, and secondly by force if force becomes necessary to this end.
>
> (Brackets in original; quoted in Palmer and Colton, 1971:490)

The Concert used force to restore the toppled Spanish and Neapolitan kings to their respective positions as sovereign authorities.

Speaking nearly 100 years later about revolutionary events in Mexico, President Woodrow Wilson said:

> There are in my judgment no conceivable circumstances which would make it right for us to direct by force or threat of force the internal processes of what is a profound revolution, a revolution as profound as that which occurred in France. All the world has been shocked ever since the time of the revolution in France that Europe should have undertaken to nullify what has been done there, no matter what the excesses.　　　　(Quoted in Gardner, 1982:27)

Yet President Wilson sent US marines to Vera Cruz, Mexico to topple the President of the provisional government, Victoriano Huerta, and he did so in the name of the sovereign people of Mexico.

Taken together, these two historical incidents point to a number of issues. They indicate that the limits of the modern international system

12

have not been historically constant. For example, in the 1820s, the reincorporation into the international community of Spain and Naples was at issue. By the 1910s, the reincorporation of Mexico was at issue. Furthermore, the types of actions that provoked armed force by one sovereign state on behalf of a government or a people of another state changed. Put in the form of a question, one might ask, was a revolution an "international" problem or was it solely a "domestic" issue? In the 1820s, the Concert of Europe viewed revolutions as international problems. By the 1910s, however, the United States officially viewed revolutions as "domestic" issues – only so long as they were liberal revolutions with the goal of putting in place a liberal, democratic government.

The domestic/international boundary became less distinct during the US invasions of Grenada and Panama in the 1980s. Similar to the Wilson Administration, the Reagan–Bush administrations viewed revolutions and/or general civil unrest as "domestic" issues. However, the US invasions of Grenada and Panama were termed "domestic" issues not because they concerned the Grenadian and Panamanian peoples but rather because they concerned the US people. Whether described as a "rescue mission" of American medical students from Grenada or as a "just cause" undertaken in the "war on drugs" in Panama, a subtle shift occurred in US intervention discourse which reinscribed US foreign policy as US domestic policy.

As these cases demonstrate, international relations was and is an arena for the contestation of meanings – meanings not just of foundational concepts like kings and people but of sovereignty, intervention, and the state. How meanings take shape and are put to work – by whom and on whose behalf – has implications for just what forms international practice legitimately can take. The examples of interventionary activity in the 1820s, 1910s and 1980s are cases in point. They bring to the fore the importance of casting meanings in particular ways which enable specific forms of practice to take place legitimately in the eyes of a supposed interpretive community.

For example, the Concert of Europe found it impossible to crush rebellions in Spain and Naples until they arrived at understandings of what the rights and duties of Concert members to other Concert members were and what the relationship was between sovereignty and intervention. This required fixing the meaning of sovereignty through intervention practices. This was so because even though intervention practices raised questions about the location of sovereign authority and the boundaries of supposed "domestic" and "international communities," intervention discourse – the justifications for intervention practices – settled these questions, however temporarily.

13

When "intervening" or "correcting" sovereign states offered justifications for their practices, they presupposed an "international community" to whom their discourse was directed and a "domestic community" for whom they spoke. Furthermore, intervention justifications elaborated the officialized rationale for what constituted a legitimate cause for interventionary behavior and under what conditions this rationale could and/or must be translated into intervention practices.

Acting in a very different political climate founded on different notions of sovereign authority (now invested in the people) and intervention, and encompassing a much larger scope and variety of states, in the 1910s Woodrow Wilson sought ways to fight for liberal democracy in Mexico and Russia without claiming a right to intervention. Quite the contrary, Wilson insisted that no such right existed. He did so in order to respect the sovereign authority of the people of Mexico and Russia. This was why, for example, he went to great lengths to assure the supposed international community as well as his legitimating "domestic community" – the American public – that he had not and would not intervene into the affairs of the Mexican people. And, in the restricted terms he inscribed the terms "intervention" and "the Mexican people," it is possible to argue that he was true to his word. But how can the sending of armed troops without invitation to a state with which the United States was not at war be anything but intervention? The answer seems to lie in what is meant by the people, sovereignty and intervention and in what the practical relationship of these concepts is at any particular historical period in any specific geographic locale.

In Wilson's case, believing that sovereign authority resided in the people was not enough. What was critical was to "invent the people"[3] in some form which could serve as the basis for US intervention in a seemingly legitimate form – a form not questioned nor condemned by the supposed international community. This explains Wilson's unlikely "discovery" of liberal democrats in counter-revolutionary Siberia during the Bolshevik Revolution. A liberal democratic people could be protected from an exclusionary, class-minded government (the Bolsheviks) by a country like the United States, a champion of universalized notions of liberal democracy.

The US invasions of Grenada and Panama in many ways appear to be updated versions of Wilsonian ideals played out in the modern era. Indeed, there is much continuity among US invasions in the 1900s. Since the Wilson era, for example, US foreign policy has retained its firmly liberal-democratic cast. Even more importantly, though, is that

US intervention discourses regularly hold that the source of sovereign authority is the people. Yet the way "the people" appeared in this discourse has changed. Rather than describing "the people" as emerging liberal-democratic capitalists, "the people" appear as statistical abstractions which do not refer back to any tangible group. In the speeches made by Presidents Reagan and Bush concerning these invasions, the Grenadian and Panamanian peoples appeared as percentage approval ratings for the invasions in public opinion polls.

Another important variation between Wilson Administration and Reagan–Bush Administration intervention discourses has to do with the constitution of interpretive communities. During the Wilson era, the interpretive community which judged the legitimacy of US intervention policies was located outside of US territorial boundaries. It was some faction of the supposed international community. A specific interpretive community was posed to render judgments about the legitimacy of intervention practices because it was regarded as an enduring, authoritative locus of international diplomatic practice regarding a particular region or activity. Thus, the Wilson Administration justified its intervention practices in Mexico primarily to European powers with ties to the Western hemisphere (the British, for example) and secondarily to Latin American states. US interventionary practices in Siberia, undertaken jointly with the Allied Powers, were justified to Allied nations.

US discourse concerning the invasions of Grenada and Panama includes intervention justifications to interpretive communities. Yet the composition of these communities is qualitatively different than it was during the Wilson era. In the case of Grenada, the interpretive community is the Organization of Eastern Caribbean States (OECS) – a regional organization that was asked by the Reagan Administration to request US assistance with a military invasion of Grenada. While this organization did exist prior to the invasion, it was not the authoritative locus of international or even regional diplomatic practice concerning the Grenada case. Other diplomatic organizations such as the United Nations or the Organization of American States were more obvious communities to judge the legitimacy of US intervention practices. That the US acted in opposition to UN and OAS recommendations and looked to the OECS for interpretive support underscored the constructedness of the OECS as an interpretive community for US purposes.[4]

The US invasion of Panama turned the search for an interpretive community inwardly. Like any intervention discourse, the Bush Administration's discourse on the Panama invasion is concerned with

15

justifying US interventionary behavior to a community of judgment that can legitimate US practices. Unlike pervious intervention discourses, however, the Panama invasion discourse finds this community of judgment at home rather than abroad. It is the US citizenry.

While it is customary for state leaders to justify intervention practices to their domestic citizenries, this discourse is always accompanied by justifications directed toward some supposed international community, and it is the international community that clarifies difficult interpretive questions about where the boundary of sovereign authority lies, where sovereign authority resides, and whether or not a particular intervention is legitimate. This is not the case with the Panama intervention discourse because the US invasion of Panama is constructed as a matter of US domestic rather than foreign policy. The Bush Administration discourse on the Panama invasion discursively "domesticates" Panama. Arguing that the US invasion of Panama was one action in the administration's "war on drugs," the Bush Administration effectively erased the domestic/international boundary that discursively separated the US from Panama and subsumed Panama within US *domestic* rather than *foreign* policy interests.

These preliminary interpretations of intervention practices illustrate the transitory character of the sovereign subjects, interpretive communities, and domestic/international boundaries. To locate sovereign authority in different political bodies; to find interpretive communities of intervention practices both outside of and within the territory of a particular state; and to construct a justification for intervening in a target state as a matter of the domestic policy of the intervening state – all these practices have an impact on what sovereignty means and on how sovereign authority might be exercised. These observations suggest that the meanings attached to sovereignty and the practices which follow from them are historically and geographically variable. And, if this is the case, then the state – that seemingly foundational entity in global politics "essentially" described by the term sovereignty – is historically and geographically variable as well.

Investigations of intervention practices have not traditionally led theorists to speculate about the variability of sovereignty. Consequently, traditional analyses of intervention practices have not reached the same conclusion. But how, in the face of abundant historical data, could analyses of intervention fail to note this slippage in the notion of sovereignty? The answer is that these studies cannot offer any unique observations about sovereignty because they begin by making sovereignty a given. A brief review of conventional approaches to the study of intervention illustrates this point.

Conventional Approaches to the Study of Intervention

As Stanley Hoffmann noted, discussions of intervention often "consist only of an endless series of classifications" (Hoffmann, 1984:7). This is so whether the topic is pursued by international lawyers – who weigh issues of legality (see, for example, Higgins, 1984) – or by international relations theorists – who modify questions of legality to those of adherence to or violation of the norm of non-intervention (see, for example, Vincent, 1974; Little, 1975). So pervasive are these tendencies in the literature on intervention that it is difficult to gain a critical distance from these familiar projects, much less to imagine an alternative approach to the investigation of intervention.

Since James Rosenau's (1968, 1969) early call for a scientific study of intervention, practitioners of behavioral social science have been preoccupied with generating a precise definition of intervention and operationalizing it to account for observed international patterns of behavior. Rosenau began by discriminating between the vague notions of intervention circulating in diplomatic practice (which elude scientific classification and measurement) and a clear conception of intervention necessary for scientific study. Generally, he defined intervention as a deviation in the relations between an intervener and a target state which is aimed at altering the authority structure in the target state (1968).

Rosenau's definition functioned as an invitation to further specify the nature of intervention rather than to settle debate on this issue. After narrowing their consideration to measurable acts of overt military intervention, behavioral social scientists embarked upon a series of distinctions in the general area of intervention.

> First, the target is differentiated: a distinction is drawn between integrated and fragmented states. Second, the intervener's objective is differentiated: a distinction is drawn between the desire to change the policy and the authority structure of the target state. Third, the instruments of the intervener are differentiated. (Little, 1987:53)[5]

This behavioralist impulse to divide and classify aspects of interventionary behavior into clearly operationalized components seems to hold that once sufficient numbers of accurate and rigorous discriminations are made to unpack the complexities inherent in interventionary behavior, the concept will reveal itself in all its transparency. What the efforts by practitioners of behavioral social science have yielded are interesting analyses of what types of behavior occur in various, highly specified situations and have raised important questions about what may or may not constitute interventionary behavior (Mitchell, 1970;

17

Pearson, 1974; Weede, 1978; Siverson and Tennefoss, 1982; Raymond and Kegley, 1987; and Gurr, 1988). What these efforts have not done, however, is uncover the "nature" of intervention, either as a general theory or as a pattern of behavior. Their failure in this respect is noteworthy not only because this is an implicit goal of behavioral analysis but more importantly because this effort is misdirected.

It is possible to ask meaningful questions about intervention by employing behavioral techniques; however, it is not possible to do so without simultaneously settling some questions about meaning. Put differently, behavioral projects which aim to "uncover" or "discover" the nature of interventionary behavior succeed only in that they create or invent the nature of interventionary behavior through the conduct of their analyses. If behavioral analysis "uncovers" or "discovers" anything, it is its own prespecified, theoretical meaning of intervention. To illustrate this point, consider the scientific behavioral method's debts to a logic of representation and to the practice of operationalization.

Scientific behavioral methods are firmly rooted in a logic of representation. According to the assumptions of these methods, it is possible to get indications of law-like regularities or patterns through the observation of direct or indirect empirical phenomena. Restated in the language of semiotics, regularities or patterns – signifieds – can be said to exist (or, more closely following Karl Popper's notion of falsification, not be said to not exist) if one can find empirical indicators of these regularities or patterns – signifiers. Thus, indicators or signifiers represent patterns or signifieds. As applied to scientific behavioral analyses of intervention, signifiers or indicators are conceptualized, differentiated from one another, operationalized, and tested to see whether or not they pertain in the highly specified cases encompassed in a particular study. For example, intervention commonly has been operationalized as "the movement of troops or military forces by one independent country, or a group of countries in concert, across the border of another independent country (or colony of an independent country), or actions by troops already stationed in the target country" (Pearson, 1974:261).

But where do indicators, signifiers, and operationalizations come from? It is theorists who impose definitions of intervention and propose indicators to capture interventionary behavior, and they do so from outside of history. That is, these definitions are not generated by historical conditions or by the cases analyzed themselves; rather, these definitions are decided prior to analysis by theorists. In the words of Richard Little, "The definition of intervention is generally established

18

by the analyst without reference to the views of the practitioner" (Little, 1987:51). And while operationalizations of intervention inform hypotheses which are tested against data to determine whether or not a given hypothesis is falsified, what is tested is not the "nature" of intervention but the meaning that theorists have given to intervention in a particular instance. In other words, meaning is generated by the theorists so that it may be tested.

Working within a logic of representation, scientific behavioral analyses seem to give indications of whether or not an operationalized meaning is valid when applied to particular data (Raymond and Kegley's analysis of the international system is a particularly good illustration of this). However, theorists must be cautious not to confuse this type of analysis – when a theoretically generated meaning applies to a data set – with analyses which ask what intervention means or how these meanings were historically constituted. Scientific behavioralists cannot ask these questions because these very questions must be settled before analysis begins. Furthermore, what constitutes an indicator or signifier of a particular behavior or signified also is determined by theorists. For example, that foreign troop movements across international borders represent interventionary behavior is established *a priori* by the theorists and is not evidence that a logic of representation works with reference to analyses of intervention; rather, it is evidence only that scientific behavioral theorists assume that it does.

Notice that in scientific behavioral approaches to the study of intervention, one begins by stabilizing the meaning of intervention, and stabilizing is done by theorists. Two assumptions are implicit in this practice of stabilization. The first is that one can refer to a stable meaning of intervention even if changes in state behavior occur. That is, referring to the operationalization of intervention just mentioned, foreign troop movements across international boundaries under specific circumstances have always been, are, and always will be regarded as interventions. The scientific behavioral project takes as its goal the clarification of intervention through scientific exploration. For this goal to be attainable, it must be held that intervention has a fixed, "essential" meaning. In this sense, the practice of operationalization can be seen as the positing of one probable meaning of intervention after another, with the ultimate hope of arriving at the "true" meaning eventually.

The second assumption is related to the first. Namely, there is an often unarticulated notion that it is possible to arrive at the "true" meaning of intervention because the meaning of sovereignty is already stabilized in international relations theory. If, as in conventional international relations theory about both sovereignty and intervention, intervention is understood to be the flip side of sovereignty, then to the extent that the meaning of sovereignty is already stabilized in international relations theory, theorists can begin to stabilize the meaning of intervention. The only questions one need ask to arrive at a stable meaning of intervention are when, how, and under what conditions sovereignty is violated. And what it means to violate sovereignty is decided by theorists when they operationalize the meaning of intervention.

Another approach to the study of intervention is variously termed traditional, normative or legal. This approach generally focuses on nonintervention as a pervasive norm in the modern international system. Nonintervention is taken as the normal state of affairs in international relations. What must be analyzed and explained, as with the behavioral approach, is intervention.

This preoccupation with norms enriches analyses of intervention because it returns practices to their historical context. For example, researchers do not abstract historical incidents into data sets and test them against operationalized definitions. Rather, the meaning of intervention is derived from historically specific cases. As Richard Little notes in his review of intervention literatures: "The idea of a static, ahistorical conception of intervention is antithetical to the traditionalist approach. Instead, traditionalists are preoccupied with conflicting conceptions of intervention and with the way the meaning of the concept can change over time" (Little, 1987:53).

However, like scientific behavioralists, the meaning of intervention is derived in reference to the meaning of sovereignty. This is illustrated in the work of R. J. Vincent. Vincent defines intervention as a violation of the norm of nonintervention. Intervention for Vincent is:

> that activity undertaken by a state, a group within a state, a group of states or an international organ which interferes coercively in the domestic affairs of another state. It is a discrete event having a beginning and an end, and it is aimed at the authority structure of the target state. It is not necessarily lawful or unlawful, but it does break a conventional pattern of international relations.   (Vincent, 1974:13)

The "conventional pattern" to which Vincent refers is the practice of nonintervention. He notes further that the principle of nonintervention is derived from the principle of sovereignty (1974:14). For Vincent, sovereignty is a "first principle." Sovereignty is the stable foundation to which analysis refers. To embark upon an investigation of intervention or violations of the norm of nonintervention, sovereignty as a "first principle" must already be in place. Treating sovereignty as a "first principle" is not unique to Vincent's work; rather, it is common practice in the traditional literature (see, for example, Little, 1975; Bull, 1984; Thomas, 1985).

Just as in the behavioral literature where sovereignty and intervention operate as conceptual opposites, so too do they operate as conceptual opposites in the normative literature. Indeed, sovereignty and intervention form the boundary of a sovereign state's authority. Vincent quotes Richard Falk on this point, who notes that nonintervention is the "doctrinal mechanism to express the outer limits of permissible influence that one state may properly exert upon another" (Falk, 1963:159). Thus, continues Vincent: "To ask what areas the principle of nonintervention protects is equivalent to asking what matters are within the domestic jurisdiction of states" (1974: 15).

The different ways in which scientific behavioralists and traditionalists deal with meaning parallel a distinction between thin and thick description applied to anthropology by Clifford Geertz. In his book *The Interpretation of Cultures*, Geertz describes how approaches to ethnography or cultural anthropology are tied to understandings and descriptions of culture. Culture, he notes, has variously been the object of "thin description" and "thick description."[6] Thin description takes as its focus of analysis observable phenomena. The aim of thin description is to derive theoretical generalizations from the testing of data or observable phenomena against hypotheses.

As applied to the study of cultures, thin description, Geertz notes has some shortcomings, and these shortcomings have to do with interpretive questions of meaning. If one focuses on observable phenomena that are abstracted from their cultural contexts, then one cannot interpret what these phenomena mean within their particular culture. This is because the same observable phenomena can have different meanings in different contexts. Take, for example, the different meanings conveyed by a wink and a twitch (Geertz, 1973:6–7). Both involve the same physical movements, and divorced from their specific performative contexts, they appear to be the same. Thin descriptions would note no differences between them. However, if one interprets a wink and a twitch in their social contexts – if one employs thick description – different meanings conveyed by identical physical movements are revealed. Unlike a twitch which is involuntary, a wink is a gesture, a signal sent to someone else. Depending on contextual criteria, this gesture many signal ridicule, conspiracy, satire, etc.

What thick description takes into account and thin description overlooks is culture. Geertz views culture as a semiotic concept. That

21

is, culture refers to a particular symbolic order, to particular signifiers referring to particular signifieds. And, explains Geertz, "[c]ulture is public because meaning is" (Geertz, 1973: 12). A semiotic approach to culture takes this public into account. As Geertz puts it, "The whole point of a semiotic approach to culture is…to aid us in gaining access to the conceptual world in which our subjects live so that we can, in some extended sense of the term, converse with them (1973: 24). To do ethnography – to study culture – one must not only note observable phenomena but attempt to gain access to different symbolic orders or cultures. Geertz says: "Doing ethnography is like trying to read (in the sense of "construct a reading of") a manuscript – foreign, faded, full of ellipses, incoherences, suspicious emendations, and tendentious commentaries, but written not in conventionalized graphs of sound but in transient examples of shaped behavior" (Geertz, 1973: 10).

Thus, ethnographic analysis – when it moves from thin description to thick description – retains its focus on behavior but for different reasons. In providing a thick description, "[b]ehavior must be attended to, and with some exactness, because it is through the flow of behavior – or, more precisely, social action – that cultural forms find articulation" (Geertz, 1973: 17).

As applied to the two conventional approaches to the study of intervention discussed here, scientific behavioral analyses employ thin description; traditionalists, thick description. By way of illustration, recall the preliminary interpretations of historical intervention practices by the Concert of Europe and the United States noted earlier. A behavioral social scientist probably would classify these episodes as indicators of interventionary behavior by testing them against an operationalized meaning of intervention indicated by uninvited troop movements across state territorial boundaries. These historical episodes would be extracted from their historical contexts in the hopes of arriving at some general theoretical propositions.

Because of their neglect of historical contexts or "international culture," scientific behavioral interpretations of these cases would be unequipped to handle a question such as: how could President Wilson maintain in 1917 that the particular practices operationalized by behavioral social scientists as intervention – the uninvited sending of United States troops to Mexico – were not an instance of intervention? Such a question raises another question – what does intervention mean in a particular historical period? Thin description as a mode of analysis employed by behavioral social scientists is unable to do anything but fall back on ahistorical, operationalized meanings of intervention. Consideration of historically generated meanings – or cracking the symbolic order of a particular international culture operating in a specific historical period – is beyond its scope.

In contrast, traditional approaches to the study of intervention employ thick description. Analyzing the very same episodes of historical practice, traditional theorists might argue for the legality or illegality of practices, or, referring to the historically changing content of norms of nonintervention, note violations of these conventional forms of behavior. Both of these kinds of traditional interpretations take historical context or "international culture" into account because they assume the existence of an "international community." What intervention means, according to traditionalists, changes as norms of nonintervention change, and these norms are interpreted by a supposed international community. Thus, meanings of intervention are not imposed from beyond history by theorists but are generated through historical practices. And, without reference to some extrahistorical definition, intervention is meaningful in international practice so long as there is a supposed international community to interpret the norms of nonintervention.[7] Symbolic orders which convey meanings in particular historical periods can be examined by traditionalists. Thus, traditionalists can offer interpretations of why United States troop movements into Mexico in 1917 may not have violated international norms of nonintervention and therefore might not have been instances of intervention.

Adopting the gaze of a cultural anthropologist when assessing conventional approaches to the study of intervention, questions of meaning gain critical importance. From such a perspective, traditional approaches to the study of intervention promise richer analyses than do scientific behavioral approaches. Given this, it might be suggested that if one is interested in questions of meaning, one should conduct analyses of intervention cases by employing traditional methods. I want to suggest that while traditional approaches do enrich analyses of intervention, they do not go far enough. While traditional approaches treat questions of meaning differently than do scientific behavioral approaches, both approaches share similar debts and thus restrictions.

In particular, as Little (1987) mentions in his review of the intervention literature, when one speaks of boundaries between interventions practices and sovereignty, one is speaking of the state. He concludes that both scientific behavioral and traditional investigations of intervention have not offered more to international relations because they are restricted by prevailing theorizations of the state in international relations. In Little's view, "According to this theory [of international relations], states are defined as sovereign institutions which possess absolute authority over their own territory. Any erosion of this authority is considered to challenge the sovereignty and, therefore, the existence of the state (Little, 1987:54).[8]

In making this argument, Little highlights the importance of theorizing about the state when one investigates sovereignty and intervention. He argues that international relations theories of the state must improve for intervention analyses to improve (1987:59). However, what Little does not recognize is that refining a theory of the state is just what these approaches to the study of intervention *cannot* do because they begin by positing the state as sovereign and then use sovereignty as a point of reference.[9]

Recall once again the preliminary interpretations of historical intervention practices by the Concert of Europe and the United States noted earlier. Conventional interpretations of these historical incidents would focus on intervention as a violation of state sovereignty. A behavioral social scientist would use an operationalized definition of intervention as his interpretive guide; a traditional theorist would use social codes of legality or nonintervention as her interpretive guide.

What both conventional approaches presuppose are sovereign states with boundaries that might be violated. It is the job of conventional theorists to determine under what conditions the boundaries of sovereign states are violated. It is beyond the scope of their analyses to question what the boundaries of sovereign states are, what constitutes a sovereign state, and whether or not it is possible to speak of sovereign states. For these conventional interpretations of intervention to be meaningful, there must already exist domestic communities whose authority can be violated and (for normative interpretations) international communities who can judge whether or not intervention norms have been violated.

For domestic communities to exist, two conditions must be met. First, one must solve problems of inclusion and exclusion. That is, who is and is not a member of any domestic community must be clear. Thus, a domestic community must be distinguishable both from members of other domestic communities and others who are not members of any community. As the illustrations of intervention practices at the beginning of this chapter indicate, distinguishing just who is and is not a member of a domestic community is never easy, particular in times of domestic turmoil. Who was a member of the domestic community in Spain in 1820 or of Mexico in 1917? In the face of this difficulty, both approaches to the study of intervention meet the condition of distinguishing a domestic community theoretically.

24

Both approaches hold that sovereignty and intervention constitute the boundary of sovereign authority for a state. Yet in both cases, this boundary is stabilized by theorists and not by international practice. For scientific behaviorialists, this boundary is drawn in the act of operationalizing intervention in relation to state sovereignty. For traditionalists, this boundary is drawn by stabilizing sovereignty as a "first principle" and, while holding sovereignty constant, asking what intervention means in relation to prevailing norms of nonintervention.

A second condition which must be met for one to speak of "domestic communities" is for the transitory character of sovereign authority to be overlooked. That is, theorists cast a blind eye toward practices which displace monarchical sovereignty with popular sovereignty and to the various representations of popular sovereignty. Theorists of both approaches cannot and indeed must not acknowledge that foundations of sovereign authority change historically. One cannot acknowledge that the meanings of both sovereignty and intervention change historically if the meaning of one depends upon the meaning of the other. For to acknowledge the variable content in that which one holds constant – sovereignty – is to prevent analysis of intervention.

Additionally, both approaches reserve a site of judgment. At this location, answers to whether or not a specific practice is an instance of intervention are given. For scientific behavioralists, answers are pronounced by theorists. Theorists are the site of judgment. For traditionalists, however, the site of judgment is a supposed international community. In his book on intervention, Little notes the interdependence of the concepts of international society and nonintervention norms:

> The purpose of international norms ... is to assist in the development and maintenance of an ordered international society ... [States] abide by the norms to promote this order. One of the cardinal rules which underlies the conception of an international society is the nonintervention norm. It is on the basis of this norm that the sovereignty and independence of states are maintained ... Without a conception of international society, a basic principle of this kind cannot function.
>
> (1978:18)

Little's point is that it is an interpretive community – in this case a supposed international community – which gives meaning to international norms. Without an interpretive community, norms cannot function because no one can authoritatively say what norms mean. And, like domestic communities, for international communities to exist requires both stable domestic/international boundaries and clear constituencies (this time of sovereign states rather than of citizens). As

25

already noted, these boundaries and constituencies are posited *a priori* by theorists.

Reconsidering statehood

Taking these points together, it seems that if one attends seriously to Little's call for a reconsideration of theories of sovereign statehood, one might begin by analyzing the relationship between sovereignty and intervention. If sovereignty and intervention in some sense constitute a boundary, then the interesting question is what does this boundary mean in international practice? How is it constituted in practice and what are its implications for the state? Asking such questions requires breaking with both scientific behavioral and traditional approaches to the study of intervention because both approaches treat boundaries as accomplished facts rather than as open questions which find temporary solutions in international practice.

Furthermore, both approaches are rooted in a logic of representation which allows one to treat sovereignty and intervention as signified and signifier. However a symbolic order is generated – by theorists positioned outside of history or by practitioners positioned within history – within a symbolic order, signifiers represent signifieds. For scientific behavioralists, that intervention signifies a violation of sovereignty is worked out through theoretical practices of operationalization.

For traditionalists, intervention also signifies a violation of sovereignty. Yet in contrast to scientific behavioralists, traditionalists do allow for variable meanings of intervention at different historical periods. What intervention means, according to traditionalists, changes as norms of nonintervention change. For traditionalists, meanings of intervention are not generated by theorists but by a supposed international community. Thus, as noted above, that meanings are public, worked out in practice, and historically interpreted so that the same observable phenomena can carry different meanings in different cultures, is accounted for in traditional approaches. However, regardless of its specific meaning, intervention is meaningful only in relation to norms of nonintervention, and these norms are only meaningful in relation to sovereignty.[10]

To work within a logic of representation is to maintain that a foundation or signified exists to ground speech. With respect to intervention, this presumed ground is sovereignty. Intervention is a meaningful concept so long as it expresses a violation of state sovereignty. But what happens – as in the cases of revolutionary states –

26

when one cannot meaningfully speak of state sovereignty? What happens when state boundaries cannot be stabilized, domestic communities cannot be identified, and a transference of authority from a citizenry to a state government cannot take place? With respect to this ambiguously specified locale, is it possible to speak of sovereignty, much less a violation of state sovereignty? Put simply, can one meaningfully speak of states, sovereignty, and intervention practices in the absence of clear foundations?

The answer seems to be both yes and no. That theorists regularly speak about states, sovereignty, and intervention as if these concepts refer back to some foundation or ground has two important effects. First, to speak about intervention practices is to imply the existence of sovereign states. This might be called the alibi function of discourses of intervention. According to Jean Baudrillard, one way to assert the existence of something (sovereignty) is to insist upon the existence of its opposite (intervention). As noted earlier, for intervention to be a meaningful concept, sovereignty must exist because intervention implies a violation of sovereignty. To speak of intervention, then, is to suggest that sovereignty does exist. "Intervention" functions as an alibi for "sovereignty."

The second effect of speaking about states, sovereignty, and intervention as if they refer back to a foundation or signified is to constitute foundations in the very act of speaking about "them." Often, this presumed ultimate signified is a domestic citizenry. And while no stable citizenry – no domestic community within clear, fixed boundaries – can be located in practice, speaking as if a stable citizenry exists is to fix (however temporarily) the content of that citizenry discursively. It is through discursive practices that foundational meanings are identified and, thanks to this act of stabilization, sovereign states are "written" or constituted.

What is at stake in the contestation of meaning in discourses of sovereignty and intervention is the sovereign state. I suggest that there is no "natural" sovereign state because there is no "natural" foundation of sovereignty. While the belief that sovereign authority resides in "the people" has become a less and less questioned foundation of state authority in the modern state system, this fact does not settle debates about sovereignty because just who the people are and who legitimately can speak for them is contested and constructed daily in international practice. And very often, debates about who "the people" are and where sovereign authority resides occur around episodes of intervention practices.

For the foundational myth of the sovereign state to be believable, the

27

state requires more than a creation myth justifying its authority. What must be done to effect a sovereign state is to control how its people are "written" or constituted – how their meaning is fixed. This is no small task. A state does not always monopolize control of the meanings of its mystical source of authority. Indeed, this power often has been claimed effectively by one or more other "intervening" or "correcting" sovereign state – acting on behalf of the international community or on behalf of some universalized principle of man (man as liberal democratic citizen, for example) – which penetrates the sovereign sphere of the state in the very name of sovereignty. This practice is justified by reference to the source of sovereign authority in the penetrated state (the king or the people) and by the interfering states' claim to represent that source.

Amidst competing versions which claim to speak on behalf of the source of sovereign authority, states are "written" or constituted in two ways. First, states are "written" effects of attempts to exert effective control over representation, both political and symbolic. If a state is unable politically or symbolically to represent its people, then it risks losing its source of sovereign authority. It therefore risks losing the legitimacy attached to its claim to speak for its source of sovereign authority in international affairs. Only by maintaining control over the depiction of its people can the state authoritatively claim to be the agent of its people. Without the ability to make credible its claims to both political and symbolic representation, the state risks forfeiting its presumed ability of representation and ultimately its sovereignty.

Secondly, competing claims to speak on behalf of the sovereign authority of a state not only "write" or invent the foundational authorities of states but also "write" or draw boundaries between that which is within the sovereign jurisdiction of the state and that which is beyond it. If, for example, a state experiencing domestic turmoil can no longer write its "people," then another sovereign state may claim to speak for the sovereign authority within this divided state. This is what President Wilson did in both the Mexican and Bolshevik revolutions. Making distinctions between governments and peoples, Wilson claimed to speak for and act on behalf of the Mexican and Russian peoples and against their respective governments. Furthermore, Wilson maintained that in the case of Mexico these practices did not constitute intervention. In so doing, Wilson redrew the boundaries of sovereign authority of Mexico and the newly forming Soviet Union.

How Wilson and others "write" foundational meanings or signifieds in relation to notions of sovereignty and intervention – signifiers in this case – redraws boundaries between sovereignty and intervention and expresses what it means to be a state at a particular time and place. If one wants to break with scientific behavioral and traditional analyses of sovereignty and intervention in a way that enriches analyses of the state, one must analyze how foundations and boundaries are drawn – how states are written (in logics of representation and logics of simulation) with particular capacities and legitimacies at particular times and places.

3 INTERPRETIVE APPROACHES

I propose to trace historically the constitution and interpretation of community standards for legitimate intervention practices and their corresponding effects upon collective understandings of state sovereignty. Sovereignty can take various forms, depending upon how it is represented or simulated and what its foundations or models are. Three central questions inform my analysis.

I begin by asking, "What is represented?" More specifically I ask: what, if any, are the reigning community-recognized standards of interpretation in terms of sovereignty and intervention justifications for the Concert of Europe, the Wilson administration, and the Reagan–Bush Administrations?; who or what is the foundational authority figure for each interpretive community?; where if anywhere does sovereignty reside in each distinct historical period and for each particular intersubjective community?; what if anything does sovereignty mean for each community?; and what does and does not count as an intervention for each community?

Representation is often taken for granted. It is the last question we consider when we think, yet the first question we ask (at least subconsciously) when we read. To lend continuity to my presentation of intervention debates in Concert of Europe, Wilson administration, and Reagan–Bush Administrations discourses, I ask "what is represented?" first to facilitate reading. I return to it again in the conclusion to facilitate a rethinking of representational logics.

My second question is, "how are sovereign foundations represented?" By way of what strategies are power and knowledge organized so that sovereign foundations are discursively constructed? How in particular do intervention justifications participate in the construction of sovereign foundations, be they domestic (citizenries) or international (interpretive communities)? Poststructuralist techniques informed by the works of Michel Foucault are employed to investigate these questions. I draw upon Foucault's three modalities of the power to punish (the mark, sign, and trace) and his analysis of the power/knowledge nexus to trace the shifting locations of sovereignty as constructed by intervention justifications.

Finally, I pose the question, "what happens when it is no longer possible to represent sovereign foundations?" In other words, what happens when a logic of representation fails and is replaced by a logic of simulation? I again employ poststructuralist techniques to address these questions; however, this time I turn to the works of Jean Baudrillard because while (like Foucault) Baudrillard identifies several symbolic orders (counterfeit, production, and simulation) and their corresponding foundations or models (god/nature, laboring man, and models), only the first two orders describe representational logics while the final one describes a post-representational logic. Using the insights found in Baudrillard's work, it is possible to analyze the relations between sovereignty and intervention after representation.

A Foucauldian approach

The scope of Michel Foucault's writings is enormous, touching on numerous subjects (science, medicine, psychology, sexuality, discipline, ethics, etc.) and employing a variety of interpretive techniques (archeology, genealogy, etc.). In this brief presentation of a Foucauldian approach, I focus on Foucault's genealogy of the power to punish and the application of three modalities of punishment (the mark, the sign, and the trace) to interpretations of intervention practices. I do so in order to raise the question, "How is representation possible?"

In *Discipline and Punish* (1979), Foucault traces the social construction of disciplinary techniques and their utilization by the state in the modern era back to earlier organizations of the power to punish found in the classical age. Each era is described in terms of the foundational authority of the body politic, the technique of punishment, the modalities of the inscription of punishment, the affected parts of the criminal's body, and the potential effects of the exercise of power on the body politic.

The classical age was the age of monarchical sovereignty in which the monarch served as the foundational authority of the body politic on earth and traced this earthly authority to god. An offense against the state, then, was an offense against the body of the monarch and of god. Torture was the technique of punishment, where the monarch's vengeance was publically inscribed on the surface of the criminal's body. While public displays of torture were designed to *mark* the criminal's body with both the criminal's transgression and the monarch's power, they occasionally had the effect of turning the

31

criminal into a martyr in the eyes of the public and encouraging resistance to monarchical excesses of the displays of power. Increasingly, tortures were concealed from public view, and eventually new, more efficient organizations of the stately power to punish displaced those of the classical age.

These new organizations of the power to punish were found in modernity, which shifts the foundation of sovereign authority from god to man and from monarchical sovereignty to popular sovereignty. The modern state was imagined as a social body which expressed the collective will of the people through citizen representatives. An offense against the modern state, then, was an offense against society or the social body. Two distinct organizations of the power to punish were found in modernity. The first might be labeled the *sign*, for punishment was inscribed on the soul of the criminal through the technique of signification. Under this system of punishment, crime and punishment were to be one thought. Instead of marking the surface of the criminal's body with the monarch's vengeance, society expressed its punishment deeper in the body. Each punishment was individualized for the criminal, who became the sign for both his particular crime (signified) and punishment (signifier). Rather than being tortured for acts of theft, arson, or poisoning, the criminal would be fined, burned, or boiled respectively. Individualizing the punishment to the crime and undertaking punishments to preserve the smooth functioning of social norms rather than to exact vengeance had the effect of decreasing the symbolic excess which accompanies acts of punishment.

The most efficient way to organize the power to punish is to avoid the necessity to punish at all. Under the final system of punishment presented by Foucault, society turned to disciplinary practices designed not only to reform criminals but also to self-discipline members of society. Through means of the *trace*, a set of habits was inscribed on the soul through techniques of reform (by example) and redemption (through work) that effectively produced self-disciplined subjects. When subjects committed a crime, traces of their old habits were recalled to put them again on the right path and new habits might be added to the old ones. The advantages of this system were enormous, for the workings of power were so thoroughly dispersed throughout society (in schools, hospitals, military services, etc.) that they were rendered virtually invisible. Resistance was thus more difficult to mobilize.

Foucault's three modalities of punishment – the mark, the sign, and the trace – correspond well to the intervention and corrective practices undertaken by the Concert of Europe, the Wilson Administration, and the Reagan–Bush Administrations respectively. The Concert of Europe – acting in the name of monarchical authority – *marked* the bodies of the deviant Spain and Naples with its power. The Wilson Administration endorsed popular sovereignty to the point of fighting for its global institutionalization. According to this administration, a nation-state must be representative – a *sign* of democratic government (signifier) acting on behalf of its citizenry (signified). Finally, the Reagan–Bush Administrations *traced* democratic traditions back to western hemispheric norms established during the Wilson Administration. The democratic ideals of the Grenadian and Panamanian peoples had to be rekindled and fortified against future threats to democracy (from Communism or drugs).

Discipline and Punish illustrates two of Foucault's central claims – that some foundational truth underwrites a particular organization of knowledge and that truth is not opposed to but is an effect of power. Elsewhere, Foucault writes:

> in a society such as ours, but basically in any society, there are manifold relations of power which permeate, characterise and constitute the social body, and these relations of power cannot themselves be established, consolidated nor implemented without the production, accumulation, circulation and functioning of a discourse. There can be no possible exercise of power without a certain economy of discourses of truth which operates through and on the basis of this association. We are subjected to the production of truth through power and we cannot exercise power except through the production of truth. (1980a:93).[1]

Foucault's analyses of the workings of power/knowledge amount to an answer to the question, "how is representation possible?" An analysis of the workings of power/knowledge does not attempt to uncover preexisting truths buried in texts or interpretive communities. Rather, it recognizes that the question "what is represented?" may preclude the Foucauldian question "how is representation possible?"

In this respect, a Foucauldian approach poses a series of questions which highlight how a search for meaning diverts attention from the production of meaning. A Foucauldian approach asks: how is truth produced by diplomatic and scholarly communities of judgment and how is truth (a sovereign foundation or a community) represented? More specifically: how, through the diplomatic and scholarly interpretive practices surrounding sovereignty and intervention, is membership in any interpretive community decided?; how, in other words, are interpretive communities effects of discourses of truth and the workings of power?; how are foundational authority figures and their locations effects of community judgments about the meanings of sovereignty and intervention?; and similarly, how are the reigning community standards of what does and does not count as intervention inscribed through historical practices of community interpretations?; finally, what does displacement of one sovereign foundation (monarchical sovereignty) with another (popular sovereignty) tell us about various representations of the state?

A Baudrillardian approach

"What happens when representation is no longer possible?" What happens when it is no longer possible to produce a truth? These are questions not considered by Foucault. The question "what is represented?" is firmly embedded in a logic of representation and presumes that meanings are recovered not produced. And while Foucault describes how representational systems are produced, he does not consider post-representational ones.[2] Beginning with his work on simulation, Jean Baudrillard explores symbolic orders after representation.

In "Symbolic Exchange and Death" (1988), Baudrillard characterizes various orders of simulation according to their laws of value. These laws of value, while derived differently,[3] bear a striking resemblance to the transcendental signifieds of Foucault's three orders of punishment – the mark, the sign, and the trace. Not only are some values or foundations the same but they also serve the same purpose, to guarantee the exchange of meaning within a symbolic order. Baudrillard's first two orders of simulation are representational orders which correspond almost exactly to Foucault's mark and sign but which have been recoded according to Baudrillard's terminology of symbolic exchange. Baudrillard's third order, however, departs from representational logics and employs a logic of simulation. It could not be described as a simple recoding of Foucault's trace.

Baudrillard labels the first order the *counterfeit*, spanning from the Renaissance to the industrial revolution. God is the transcendental signified of this order, for god is the creator of nature, and natural law underwrites this system of exchange. In this sense, Baudrillard's counterfeit is much like Foucault's mark. A sovereign is either authentic because his or her authority flows from god or a sovereign is a pretender to the throne. Sovereign authority comes to a monarch from above (god) and not from below (his or her subjects). Concert of Europe interventions in Spain and Naples can be regarded as attempts to preserve monarchical sovereignty and natural law from pretenders and liberal movements from below.

The second order, *production*, describes the dominant scheme of the industrial era. In this order, commodities are exchanged and guarantee value. Commodities can guarantee value only so long as they are exchanged within a system of equivalences. In other words, commodities must exchange for other commodities of equal value. This is very much like Foucault's characterization of punishment under the sign (burn an arsonist, execute a murderer, etc.). The emphasis on reproduction during the industrial era made this type of exchange possible. Equivalent commodities were produced, reproduced and exchanged for one another. During this era, labor was also commodified. One laborer's productive power could be measured, converted, and exchanged for the productive power of another laborer.

Political systems can be described in terms of Baudrillard's productive order. A new political code began to organize political institutions after the French Revolution. The idea that sovereign authority flowed from god and was invested in a monarch was replaced by the idea that sovereign authority flowed from the citizenry of a nation-state and was invested in its leaders. Nation-states were reproduced in various locales from this time on. The nation-state was like any other commodity form found in a productive order. According to international law, every nation-state was sovereign and therefore enjoyed equal legal privileges and responsibilities. The production of a nation-state was based on another equivalence – that of every one of its citizens. Citizens, in this sense, are like laborers in an order of production. And, as they do according to Foucault's characterization of punishment under the sign, citizens function as transcendental signifieds, as the productive foundations of meaning within political systems. The Wilson Administration's interventions in the Mexican and Bolshevik revolutions might be characterized as productive orders. The US attempted to reproduce "equivalent" democratic institutions in Mexico and Siberia and guarantee their legitimacy with reference to the peoples (who were also produced) of each emerging nation-state.

Foucault and Baudrillard part company concerning their third orders because for Foucault, this order is representational while for Baudrillard it is postrepresentational.[4] According to Baudrillard, Foucault has refined our understanding of power within a system of representation. Baudrillard describes Foucault's reconceptualization of power as follows: "it substitutes a negative, reactive, and transcendental conception of power which is founded on interdiction and law for a positive, active, and immanent conception ..." (Baudrillard, 1987a: 17).

35

Foucault's work on sexuality, madness, medicine, and discipline lead him to the conclusion that power did not work through repression. Rather, power was productive. Foucault's move from the "'despotic' to the 'disciplinary'" (Baudrillard, 1987a: 12) levels of power account for power's transition from a negative to a positive term. However, as Baudrillard observes, power as theorized by Foucault requires some term – negative or positive – to which it can refer. For power, the term of reference is always some type of truth. On Foucault's notion of power, Baudrillard observes:

> Power, then, is still turned toward a reality principle and a very strong truth principle; it is still oriented toward a possible coherence of politics and discourse (power no longer pertains to the despotic order of what is forbidden and of the law, but it still belongs to the objective order of the real). Foucault can thus describe to us the successive spirals of power, the last of which enables him to mark its most minute terminations, although power never ceases being the term, and the question of its extermination can never arise.
>
> (Baudrillard, 1987a: 12)

Moving from a negative to a positive term is like moving from repression to liberation. While the observation that power is allied with a positive term rather than a negative term in the modern era is an important one, it does not go far enough because, according to Baudrillard, there is no difference between domination and liberation, repression and production, because "any form of liberation is fomented by repression" (Baudrillard, 1987a: 26). No matter what side of this dichotomy power allies itself with, power remains within a system of representation. For Foucault, "everything still comes back to *some kind of* power" (Baudrillard, 1987a: 39): "with Foucault power remains, despite being pulverized, a *structural* and a polar notion with a perfect genealogy and an inexplicable presence, a notion which cannot be surpassed in spite of a sort of latent denunciation, a notion which is whole in each of its points or microscopic dots" (Baudrillard, 1987a: 39).

What enables Foucault's notion of power to be polar and ever-present is Foucault's theory of the object. Foucault's object remains a semiological notion. As such, it has a place within a system of representation. The object may serve as a point of reference within a symbolic order. In other words, Foucault's theory of power depends upon some real object, signified, or referent which makes meaning possible. The referent may well be recognized as a discursive effect; nevertheless, a representational system of meaning would break down if there were no referent. For Foucault, this referent is "truth."

But according to Baudrillard, representation has already broken down and been replaced by simulation. Simulation follows a structural law of value in which models of the real replace natural or produced referents. It is a matter "of substituting signs of the real for the real itself" (Baudrillard, 1983a: 4). Models are neither authentic (referring to a natural signified) nor functional (referring to a produced signified). Instead, they are self-referential, infinitely substitutable, and reversible. Given this, questions of what is "real" and what is "imaginary" have no meaning in a logic of simulation because "opposite" terms can be substituted for one another.

Baudrillard notes that simulation is particularly troubling for Western culture:

> All of Western faith and good faith was engaged in this wager on representation: that a sign could refer to the depth of meaning, that a sign could *exchange* for meaning and that something could guarantee this exchange – God,[5] of course. But what if God himself can be simulated, that is to say, reduced to the signs which attest his existence? Then the whole system becomes weightless; it is no longer anything but a gigantic simulacrum: not unreal, but a simulacrum,[6] never again exchanging for what is real, but exchanging in itself, in an uninterrupted circuit without reference or circumference.
>
> (Baudrillard, 1983a: 10–11)

While Foucault's theory of power/knowledge gives an account of the production of an object (truth) which can function in representational discourse as a transcendental signified, this is beside the point. Because symbolic exchange takes place within a system not of representation but of simulation, a theory of the object must contain a theory not of a transcendental signified or ultimate referent but of a simulacrum. A simulacrum is "a truth effect that hides the truth's non-existence" (Baudrillard, 1990: 35):

> Foucault unmasks all the final or causal illusions concerning power, but he does not tell us anything *concerning the simulacrum of power itself*. Power is an irreversible principle of organization because it fabricates the real (always more and more of the real), effecting a quadrature, nomenclature, and dictature without appeal; nowhere does it cancel itself out, become entangled in itself, or mingle with death. In this sense, even if it has no finality and no last judgment, power returns to its own identity again as a *final principle*: it is the last term, the irreducible web, the last tale that can be told; it is what structures the indeterminate equation of the word.
>
> (Baudrillard, 1987a: 40)

While Foucault contributes much to our understanding of power, he does not follow through on the implications of the productive aspect of power. Foucault recognizes that terms of reference are discursive effects; however, his theory of power requires terms of reference. Foucault can only theorize production within representational terms. Production is about representation, in which real referents have real values. And, like any representational system, production is ultimately transparent. Indeed, production "means to render visible, to cause to appear and be made to appear" (Baudrillard, 1987a: 21). What Foucault's theory of power/knowledge cannot do is explain symbolic exchange within a system that has no ultimate referents, no truth, or (and this is the same thing) so many signs of the truth that truth has no meaning. To account for this type of symbolic exchange, Baudrillard moves beyond production and representation to seduction and simulation.

While production and Foucault's productive power are linked to representation because, in their quest to render all things visible, production and productive power attempt to make meaning transparent, seduction "withdraws something from the visible order and so runs counter to production" and to representation (Baudrillard, 1987a: 21). Seduction is not concerned with "truth" but with the manipulation of appearances. Writes Baudrillard, "Seduction as a mastering of the reign of appearances opposes power as a mastering of the universe of meaning"[7] (Baudrillard, 1987b: 62). As such, seduction is of the order of simulation not representation because appearances are endlessly substituted and exchanged for one another without reference to some truth to make them meaningful. Unlike logics of representation, simulation is not concerned with true or false meanings but instead "threatens the difference between 'true' and 'false', between 'real' and 'imaginary'" (Baudrillard, 1983a: 5).

Shifting from a logic of representation to a logic of simulation, one does not ask "what is represented?" or even "how is representation possible?" Because no truth can be either uncovered or produced – therefore making representation impossible – one asks "how is the truth's non-existence concealed so that a logic of representation appears to function?" "How are images or models simulated and seduced?"

According to a Baudrillardian approach, the Reagan–Bush Administrations invasions of Grenada and Panama took place within a logic of simulation. Models of the truth (the Grenadian and Panamanian people) were manipulated or seduced in order to conceal both the truth's non-existence and the failure of representation. Investigating these invasions, I ask: if sovereign foundations could only be seduced but not produced in the discourses surrounding these invasions, what recognizable "falsehoods" were circulated as proofs of the truth's existence? What were the alibis for representation both domestically (dictators) and internationally (regional communities)? If in an order of simulation, distinctions between opposites cannot be preserved, how does this effect the relationship between sovereignty and intervention? Lacking either authentic or functional referents, might the sovereignty/intervention boundary be erased? Might sovereignty and intervention cease to function as opposed terms as they do in a logic of representation and function as interchangeable terms in an order of simulation? If so, what are the effects of this on theorizations of statehood?

Historical analyses

"What is represented?" is the first question I ask when analyzing the cases of the Concert of Europe, the Wilson Administration, and the Reagan–Bush Administrations. I then read the Concert of Europe and Wilson Administration cases through Foucault's question "how is representation possible?", paying particular attention to how, in Foucault's terms, the Concert *marked* the political bodies of Spain and Naples and the Wilson Administration attempted to disseminate the *sign* of liberal-capitalist democracy in Mexico and Siberia.[8] Concerning the Reagan–Bush Administration invasions of Grenada and Panama, I ask all three questions: what is represented?; how is representation possible?; and what happens when representation fails? In these cases, I turn to both Foucault's notion of the *trace* and Baudrillard's accounts of simulation and seduction. In the concluding chapter, I rethink the question "what is represented?" from the perspective of simulation and speculate on what it means for international relations theory to simulate sovereignty.

4 CONCERT OF EUROPE
INTERVENTIONS IN SPAIN
AND NAPLES

> Invention is the enemy of history which knows only discovery, and only that which exists can be discovered.
> Metternich[1]

When representing the sovereign authority within a state, who is to be represented? Prior to the French Revolution, questions pertaining to the legitimate foundation of stately authority did not arise for, as all knew, the sole authority of the sovereign state was the monarch. Dynastic sovereignty held sway over continental Europe as late as 1789. Yet by 1787, this self-evident truth which needed no elaboration or justification became the subject of formal pronouncement, as illustrated by a speech made by King Louis XVI's Keeper of the Seals to the French Parliament:

> These principles, universally recognized by the Nation to be true, attest that to the King alone belongs the Sovereign power in his kingdom;
> That he is accountable only to God for the exercise of the supreme power;
> That the bond uniting the King and the Nation is by nature indissoluble;
> That interests and duties that are reciprocal between the King and his subjects do nothing else than to assure the perpetuity of this union;
> That the Nation's interests require that the rights of its Chief suffer no alteration;
> That the King is Sovereign Chief of the Nation and one with the Nation;
> Finally, that the legislative power resides in the person of the Sovereign, independently and without partition.
> Gentlemen, such are the unchanging principles of the French Monarchy ...
> (Speech made on 19 November 1787, quoted in Beik, 1970:2).

Just two years later, Emmanuel Joseph Sièyes in his famous pamphlet "What is the Third Estate?" equated common citizens with the nation.

The Third [Estate] therefore includes everything that belongs to the nation; and everything not of the Third cannot be regarded as being of the nation. What is the Third? Everything ...

The Third Estate must be understood to mean all the citizens who belong to the common order. Everyone privileged by law, in whatever manner, is not of the common order, takes exception to the common law, and consequently does not belong to the Third Estate. As we have already said, a common law and a common representation are what make *one* nation ...

(Brackets in original; quoted in Beik, 1970:19).

Building on Sièyes' idea that the Third Estate – consisting of the common people – is identical to the nation, the Declaration of the Rights of Man and Citizen equated the nation with sovereignty: "The principle of all sovereignty rests essentially in the nation. No body and no individual may exercise authority which does not emanate from the nation expressly" (quoted in Lefebvre, 1947).

Where then did sovereignty reside after the French Revolution? Two locations competed as the legitimate sovereign foundations of the newly emerging nation-state – the monarch and the citizenry. Traditionally, international relations scholars have neglected to explore how struggles to establish, preserve, and displace sovereign foundations change the conduct of diplomacy, much less what these practices imply for theories of the state. Wrote noted scholar René Albrecht-Carrie of the shift from monarchical to popular sovereignty: "The subsequent course of political evolution shifted the locus of sovereignty from the ruler to the people, but this modification within the state left unaffected the claim to sovereignty vis-a-vis the outside" (1968:2).

I take a very different position. Some international practices – like intervention – are justified in terms of sovereignty. Therefore, *who is represented* as the sovereign authority within a state has implications for how diplomacy among states is carried out. If, for example, one state claims that sovereign authority is shared by the monarch and the citizenry while another state argues that monarchical sovereignty is absolute, the two states threaten one another's foundational principles. Indeed, their co-existence could become a threat to the international order. It was just these types of dilemmas over sovereign representation which occurred during the short duration of the Concert of Europe. These debates were intertwined with questions about how to conduct diplomacy. I examine Concert of Europe justifications pertaining to the interventions in Spain and Naples to *uncover* who could legitimately be represented as a state's sovereign authority and who could judge the legitimacy of sovereignty claims.

41

The Concert of Europe

The Concert of Europe was formally constituted in the Quadruple Alliance of November 20, 1815. Its members were those powers which defeated Napoleon (Austria, Prussia, Russia, and Great Britain), and its announced purpose was to guard this newly formed order, particularly from challenges that might be made by France.[2] British Foreign Secretary Castlereagh, arguing his case in favor of a Concert before Parliament in May, 1815, noted that for order to be maintained in Europe, a formal alliance system was necessary to enforce a "comprehensive system of Public Law" in Europe.

> Much will undoubtedly be effected for the future repose of Europe by these Territorial Arrangements, which will furnish a more effectual Barrier than has before existed against the ambition of France. But *in order to render this Security as complete as possible, it seems necessary*, at the point of a general Pacification, *to form a Treaty to which all the principle Powers of Europe should be Parties*, fixed and recognized, *and they should all bind themselves mutually to protect and support each other*, against any attempt to infringe them – It should re-establish a general and comprehensive system of Public Law in Europe, and Provide, as far as possible, for repressing future attempts to disturb the general Tranquillity, and above all, for restraining any projects of Aggrandizement and Calamities inflicted on Europe since the disastrous era of the French Revolution.   (Quoted in Albrecht–Carrie, 1970:33)

Castlereagh's statement aptly expressed the fundamental dictates of the Concert. First, it underscored the collective nature of the Concert. The Concert was not so much a coalition of diverse sovereign states with individual interests as it was a community of sovereign states whose interests could best be achieved collectively. Concert members had already performed collectively as an informal community during their defeat of Napoleon. The formalization of these states into a Concert was merely a matter of officializing a state of affairs that already existed.

Second, the formalization of the Concert appeared to "fix" and grant "recognition" of membership or non-membership in the new European community. In other words, what political entities should and should not be included in the European system or community could be determined by evaluating any political entity's relationship with the Concert. Membership in the Concert was equated with status as a "Great Power" in the international system. Other powers which were not members of the Concert but who abided by Concert dictates also were viewed as members of the international system. Those states which did not conform to Concert policies were located somewhere beyond the European international system. These included both European states (like Spain and Naples in the early 1820s) as well as colonies and other extra-European political configurations.

Third, Castlereagh's statement conveyed the Concert's preoccupation with order and security. It was security from French aggression that led to the formation of the Concert powers as an informal community; it was the maintenance of security and order (preferably in the form of peace) that led to the formalization of the Concert.

Fourth, underlying the formalization of the Concert was a belief that common norms, interests, and modes of conduct unified members of the European system. While the felt need to defeat Napoleon was the immediate crisis that solidified the European community, common political concerns of European powers applied during times of tranquility as well as during times of crisis. It was upon these common political understandings that the "general and comprehensive system of Public Law in Europe" to which Castlereagh referred was to be built.

Fundamental among these common understandings was the concept of legitimacy. Henry Kissinger cautions that: "'Legitimacy' ... should not be confused with justice. It means no more than an international agreement about the nature of workable arrangements and about the permissible aims and methods of foreign policy. It implies the acceptance of the framework of the international order by all major powers" (1964:1).

Following Kissinger, Richard Rosecrance breaks the concept of legitimacy into two components – acceptance and content (Rosecrance, 1963:74). Rosecrance holds that acceptance is preoccupied with the form of legitimacy while content is concerned more with results than with methods (1963:75). Rosecrance argues that the doctrine of legitimacy "represented an attempt...to achieve international transformations through acceptance" (1963:73). Rosecrance explains that the acceptance aspect of legitimacy was a new innovation, contrary to Napoleon's universal and unlimited revolutionary diplomacy which was not concerned with international acceptance as well as contrary to eighteenth-century standards of diplomatic conduct which viewed acceptance as an immanent and not an explicit principle. Rosecrance says: "Legitimacy became imperative only when acceptance was in doubt, and only when revolutionary tides had challenged the old order, did it become necessary actively to seek consensus" (1963:74). Kissinger put it this way: "Principles of obligation in a period of legitimacy are taken so much for granted that they are never talked

43

about, and such periods therefore appear to posterity as shallow and self-righteous. Principles in a revolutionary situation are so central that they are constantly talked about" (1964:3). It was explicit, active acceptance that was central to the Concert because the diplomatic environment of the times raised fundamental questions about domestic and international arrangements.

Rosecrance's second component of legitimacy is content. During the 1820s, questions about what constituted the legitimate domestic social and political order (the content of legitimacy) became hotly contested issues as they became tied to justifications for intervention. Rosecrance notes: "'Intervention' of one Power in another's domestic affairs did not become commonplace until after the French Revolution; nor was it ever an essential principle of eighteenth-century diplomacy" (1963:29). For example, during the eighteenth century, "Intervention only became necessary when some Powers ceased to give serious concern to the maintenance of the system. 'Intervention' then, was more nearly a reflection of the breakdown of the balance of power system than it was an intrinsic principle of it" (1963:29). Concert members were in agreement about the meaning of the term intervention. What they debated were the justifications for intervention.

Two legitimate justifications for intervention were available to Concert members. The first was an individual right of intervention, meaning that a sovereign state could justify its intervention practices on behalf of its national interests. For example, France could argue that events in Spain threatened the French national interest and therefore required action on the part of France to return Spain to its pre-revolutionary status. The second justification for intervention was based not on individual interests but on the Concert's collective right to intervene. According to this justification, the Concert could sanction one or more of its members to intervene in a European state if that state's social order – the political and social institutions upon which it was based – was a threat to the Concert as a whole. In this case, intervention in Spain carried out by French or other troops would be justified with reference to the Concert of Europe's right of intervention. The same justifications were available to support Austrian intervention in the Neapolitan Revolution.

The first form of justification would not require the Concert as a whole to take a position on what kind of domestic social orders were legitimate; the latter form would. It was the latter form of justification – one which referred to the Concert's collective right of intervention – that was invoked to authorize French and Austrian interventions. By deciding what kind of social order would count as the legitimate social order, the Concert of Europe combined the issues of foundational authorities and intervention. Questions such as the following were debated: should the Concert specify what form of domestic order is legitimate within the European state system?; if so, who is to be represented as a member of that order?; and finally, what represents a threat to the social order, or what does it mean for a European state *not* to be sovereign? The formal answers given by the Concert to these questions were as follows. The foundational authority figure in a European sovereign state was the monarch, from whom all powers originated. The location of sovereign authority within a sovereign state was the monarch, then, *so long as the monarch's authority was absolute.* Monarchical power could not be compromised by any extraneous domestic forces. For example, a monarch could convene a parliament for purposes of council; however, monarchical power must always be granted from above (god) and never challenged from below (by subjects or the people). If monarchical power was compromised and if an existing government in a European state was the result of a revolution, then that state was not sovereign. It was located somewhere beyond the European community of sovereign states. Therefore, what a state must do to be a sovereign state was to be constructed as an absolute monarchy in accordance with principles which did not call into question the sovereign foundations of neighboring states. Importantly, it was by rendering judgments about these issues that the Concert established itself as the legitimate interpretive community regarding these concerns.

Debate by the Concert on these questions began with the Spanish Revolution in 1820 and continued until 1823.[3] In the next section, I will focus on the discourse generated mainly by the revolution in Naples. In the Foucauldian analysis which follows, I will reinterpret this discourse – asking "how was representation possible?" – in light of the discourse generated by the revolution in Spain.

Intervention in Naples

The revolution in Naples came as a shock to Concert members, especially to Austria. A few days after the outbreak of revolution in Naples, Metternich wrote: "The blood will flow in streams. A nation half-barbaric, in absolute ignorance, of boundless superstition, hot-blooded as Africans, a nation that can neither read nor write, whose last word is the dagger, such a nation offers fine material for constitutional principles!" (July 7, 1820, to Weinzirl, quoted in Schroeder, 1962:33).

45

Even more disturbing to the Austrian government than the supposed inability of the Italian people to govern themselves constitutionally was how events in Naples put into question the foundations of Austrian social and political institutions. Friedrich von Gentz, Metternich's secretary and publicist, wrote:

> In view of the general disposition of peoples, it is impossible to deny that we have arrived at one of those dark epochs where one is unable any longer to count on anything, and where a wise man must expect from day to day to see the very ground that he believed the most solid and the best supported crumble under his feet.
>
> (July 17, 1820; quoted in Schroeder, 1962:39)

This ground, it was implied, was the sovereign authority of monarchs generally and of the Austrian monarch in particular. As Austrian Ambassador to France Vincent wrote: "Everything reduces itself to a very simple consideration and calculation indeed, that of the existence of every throne" (July 27, 1820; quoted in Schroeder, 1962:39–40). And it was upon insistence of monarchical institutions throughout Austria's European sphere of influence that its foreign policy was built and its domestic tranquility insured.

Commenting on the motto of the Neapolitan Revolution, "For God, the King, and the Constitution!", a contemporary historian wrote:

> The meaning of this political watchword was only half understood by the hearers, or even, I might say, by those who uttered it, but all believed the words contained the expression of their particular desire; those who paid taxes supposed it to mean a diminution of the rates; the Liberals, liberty; the philanthropist, the public welfare; the ambitious, power; and each that which he most coveted.
>
> (Pietro Colletta, quoted in Schenk, 1967:155)

Whatever its specific content, this motto made clear the sentiments among some Neapolitans – that monarchical power was not absolute. To allow revolutionary events in Naples to go unchecked was to threaten Austrian foundations more generally. As historian Paul Schroeder expressed the issues facing Austria:

> How could Austria demand that the German governments limit themselves to purely monarchical provincial constitutions if she tolerated the very radical Spanish Constitution at Naples? Above all, how could Metternich keep other princes from submitting to revolution and other peoples from rising in revolt if the bad examples set by Ferdinand and the Neapolitans went uncorrected? If nothing was done, even the Austrian domains, quiet and secure as they were, might not be immune from the spread of the revolutionary contagion. (1962:42)

The Neapolitan Revolution itself was evidence of revolutionary contagion because it was influenced by revolutionary events in Spain, so much so that the King of Naples was forced to adopt the Spanish Constitution of 1812 (Schenk, 1967:155).

While members of the Concert were in general agreement that Austrian interests were at stake in Naples and that Austrian troops ought to be sent into Naples to crush the revolution, the justification of this action was disputed. As noted earlier, Austria could justify intervention in Naples on either of two grounds – on the basis of Austrian national interests or on the basis of the Concert's right of intervention or both. For, as will be pointed out, when Metternich succeeded in justifying Austrian intervention in Naples on the basis of the Concert's right of intervention, he did so by equating Austrian national interests with Concert interests. In this respect, then, Austria became the ideal rendition of perfect sovereignty within the Concert community.

England favored an intervention justification based on the interests of a single state – Austria – and not on the collective interests of the Concert. This was so for at least two reasons. First, England was aware of secret treaties between Austria and various Italian states which guaranteed Austrian influence in those states, to such an extent that intervention in Naples could be justified with reference to the secret Austro-Neapolitan treaty (Schroeder, 1962:47). Second, England opposed any interpretation of Concert treaties that would (1) require the Concert to take a position on what form domestic institutions could legitimately take and (2) grant the Concert a general right of intervention.

Castlereagh made England's case with reference to revolutionary events in Spain and stood by his arguments with respect to the situation in Naples. Castlereagh's case against a general right of intervention for the Concert can be traced back to his interpretation of the Treaty of Aix-la-Chapelle. Castlereagh's interpretation of the Treaty, in contrast to Tsar Alexander's reading of it, upheld the doctrine of non-intervention.[4] Castlereagh wrote:

> no Government can be more prepared than the British Government is, to uphold the right of any State or States to interfere, where their own immediate security or essential interests are seriously endangered by the internal transactions of another State. – But ... they cannot admit that this right can receive a general and indiscriminate application to all Revolutionary Movements, without reference to their immediate bearing upon some particular State or States, or be made prospectively the basis of an Alliance. – They regard its exercise as an exception to general principles of the greatest value and importance, and as one that only properly grows out of the circumstances of

the special case; but they at the same time consider that exceptions to this description never can, without the utmost danger, be so far reduced to rule, as to be incorporated into the ordinary diplomacy of States, or into the institutes of the Law of Nations.
(Circular Dispatch to British Missions at Foreign Courts, London, January 19, 1821, quoted in Albrecht-Carrie, 1968:51)

Earlier, in his State Paper of May, 1820, Castlereagh built his argument for non-intervention upon his view that the Concert did not have the authority to determine which types of social orders were legitimate and which were not. Castlereagh's position was that the Alliance was a military alliance with a specific charge – to check French revolutionary tendencies. "It [the Alliance] never was, however, intended as an union for the government of the world or for the superintendence of the internal affairs of other States" (Castlereagh quoted in Webster, 1958:238). Castlereagh's position, then, was that the Concert was not the appropriate community to judge the legitimacy of the representation of social orders. Rather, social and political representation were issues for individual states to decide for themselves.[5]

Metternich's position was that events in Naples threatened Austrian national interests by challenging the foundation of sovereign authority – that of absolute monarchy – which was common to all the continental powers except France. Thus, it was not only preservation of the special influence Austria exercised in Italy that was at stake; it was the general order of Europe that was at stake. To Metternich, events in Naples demanded a Concert decision on what form of domestic social order was legitimate. If the Concert failed to address this question, then the larger European order would be put at risk. Drawing upon this logic while attempting to decouple Britain's position on Spain from its position on Naples, Metternich argued to Castlereagh that the Spanish and Neapolitan revolutions were of a very different character. The Spanish Revolution – a revolt against an inept monarch taking place at the periphery of Europe – could more easily be contained by a power (say France) acting individually. Events in Naples, in contrast, posed a more general challenge to European order. Metternich along with representatives of Prussia and Russia made their rationale for intervention clear in a post-intervention circular.

Europe knows the motives for the resolution taken by the Allied Sovereigns to stifle the Conspiracies, and to put an end to the Disturbances which threatened the existence of that General Peace...
the authors of those disturbances [in Naples]...[by] putting in the

place of known duties arbitrary and indefinite pretexts of a universal change in the constitutive principles of Society, they prepare for the world unending calamities.

(Declaration of the Allied Sovereigns of Austria, Prussia, and Russia, on the breaking up of the Conferences of Laybach, after the Suppression of the Revolutions in the Two Sicilies and Sardinia, May 12, 1821; reproduced in Albrecht-Carrie, 1968:56)

Thus, just as Castlereagh argued that the Concert could not survive if it took a position on legitimate domestic social orders, Metternich implied that the European order could not survive if no position were taken. This point was emphasized by Metternich in numerous documents. For example, in a Circular of the Austrian Government to the different Courts of Germany, Metternich wrote:

> The recent events in Naples have proven, with greater force than any previous occurrence, that even in a state administered with steadiness and wisdom, and inhabited by a people which is tranquil, temperate and satisfied with its government, the venom of revolutionary sects can produce violent upheavals, and bring about catastrophe. (July 25, 1820, translated by C. King; BFSP,[6] vol. 8:1,130)

Metternich went on to say that "seditious movements...caused the King of Naples to abdicate the government, dissolve existing authorities, and to proclaim a foreign constitution in his country, and thus to turn anarchy into law" (July 25, 1820, trans. by C. King; BFSP, vol. 8:1,130).

It was up to the Concert of Europe to prevent the spread of "anarchy" in the form of "law." Summing up events of the Congress of Troppau and echoing Metternich's logic, Nesselrode (a Russian Minister) wrote:

> the Cabinets assembled at Troppau could not consider the Revolution of Naples an isolated incident, they recognized the same spirit of chaos which has threatened the world for so long; which we believed we could contain by means of a general peace, but which unfortunately arose again in more than one European state, reappearing under less frightening but more essentially dangerous forms. The Sovereigns thus remained convinced that by reestablishing order in the Kingdom of Sicily [Naples], they were working for the peace and happiness of Europe.
> (January, 1821, trans. by C. King; Circular to the Austrian, Prussian and Russian Ministers; BFSP, vol. 8:1,166)

He continued:

> [T]he Sovereign Allies ... determined never to recognize a Revolution produced by crime, which could at any moment disturb the peace of the entire world, but instead to unite to end the upheavals

which threatened not only the countries they hit directly, but all countries.

(January 1821, trans. by C. King; *BFSP*, vol. 8:1,167)

At the Congress of Troppau, the Concert equated the effects of the French Revolution with the effects of revolutions against absolute monarchies generally. A Circular offering a brief summary of the first results of the conference at Troppau illustrates this.

> Everything added to the hope that this Alliance, created in critical circumstances, brilliantly successful, affirmed by the Conventions of 1814, 1815, and 1818, just as it had created and strengthened the peace of the world, and delivered the European Continent from the military tyranny of the representative of the Revolution, could also halt a force no less tyrannical and detestable, that of revolt and crime.
> (December 18, 1820, trans. by C. King; *BFSP*, vol. 8:1,149–50)

In this passage, "the representative of the Revolution" refers to Napoleon. The "military tyranny" attributed to Napoleon's conquest of Europe was the same "tyrannical and detestable" force as that embodied in the Neapolitan and Spanish revolutions.

The Circular continued:

> The Powers exercised their indisputable right, in employing security measures in the states in which the revolutionary overthrow of a government could only be considered a dangerous example, one which could result in a hostile attitude toward all legitimate Constitutions and Governments. The exercise of the right became even more urgent, when those who had placed themselves in this position sought to spread their misfortune to neighboring states, and to propagate all around them rebellion and confusion.
>
> In this attitude and behavior we can see the breakdown of the pact which guarantees to all European governments, not just the inviolability of their Territory, but also the enjoyment of peaceful relations which exclude encroachments on one another's rights.
> (December 18, 1820, trans. by C. King; *BFSP*, vol. 8:1,150)

This part of the Circular implied that "legitimate Constitutions and Governments" were those granted by monarchs and not those demanded by peoples. Therefore, when the Circular spoke of the Concert's duty to "exclude encroachments on one another's rights," these rights were those of each monarch.

The Circular concluded:

> there is no need for further proof that neither the desire for conquest, nor the desire to threaten the independence of governments in internal matters, nor the plan to prevent the carrying out of wise improvements, freely undertaken and compatible with the interests

of Peoples, had any part in the Powers' resolution. They only wish to maintain peace and to deliver Europe from the scrounge of Revolution, and to banish the evils which result in the violation of all principles of order and morality.

The Allied Monarchs believe they have the unanimous support of the world in this respect.

(December 18, 1820, trans. by C. King; *BFSP*, vol. 8:1,151)

In this section of the Circular, a distinction was made between what was "compatible with the interests of Peoples" and what was not. It was implied that "the scrounge of Revolution" is not in the interest of the people because revolution violated "all principles of order and morality." This was so because order and morality could only be secured if monarchies were safe from threats from below. A similar argument was made by Nesselrode. He commented that once the revolution in Naples was crushed, "the Allies will have but one wish – that of seeing the King almost choke at the memory of this disastrous period, and establish in his states an order which guarantees stability, is in accord with the real interests of his people, and which reassures neighboring states about their safety and future tranquility" (January, 1921, trans. by C. King; *BFSP*, vol. 8:1,167–8).

Of particular interest in this passage is Nesselrode's presumed insight as to "the real interests of his [the King of Naples'] people." One gets the impression that what the people of Naples really wanted was identical to what the Concert wanted – order, stability, and security.

At this point it should be clear that not only did Metternich and other Eastern European diplomats argue that the Concert as a whole must decide what kind of domestic social order was legitimate but also that this decision had already been made. Not surprisingly, the diplomats who represented absolute monarchies argued that absolute monarchy was the only legitimate form of domestic social order in Europe.

Metternich refined this position on behalf of the Concert. A legitimate government, according to Metternich, fulfilled two requirements. First, it regarded the monarch as the only legitimate source of sovereign authority within any state. Second, it rested upon stable institutions which insure that monarchical power would not be compromised by a revolution. In a document entitled "Points" which Metternich prepared for the Congress of Troppau, Metternich outlined what would constitute a legitimate government in post-revolutionary Naples.

The reorganization of the Kingdom must offer the strongest possible guarantees of internal stability. The *good* must in this connection be sought and attained, but it must not and cannot proceed except from the legal source of all good, from the legitimate sovereign authority.

The good which proceeds from a false basis (and such a case can happen in times of upheaval) is a very real evil for the entire society. It encourages the factious, not in this respect, that they search for the good, but rather because the deceitful appeal of the good delivers over them virtuous men and makes them their accomplices. Thus the organization most favorable to the true well-being of the Kingdom of Naples, if it was simply the immediate and direct consequence of the criminal enterprise of the factions who have leagued themselves together for the overthrow of their country, would have to be regarded as an immense evil for Europe. There is not a single state which would not feel the result of such a combination of things.
(November 15, 1820; quoted in Schroeder, 1962:75–6; italic in Schroeder)

What was good for Naples, according to Metternich, was good for Europe. Elaborating on how to construct such a legitimate government in Naples, Metternich continued:

The King, once free, will have to assure the future of his Kingdom. He must to this effect,
a) Consult the true needs of his country.
These needs are composed, at Naples as everywhere else, of the strong and sustained action of the government and of guarantees which institutions suitable to the national character can offer, guarantees suitable at once to prevent the authority of government from going astray and the subjects from infringing on the authority.
b) Establish and regulate the form of his administration in a way which would not be in opposition to the internal tranquillity of neighboring states.
(November 15, 1820; quoted in Schroeder, 1962:76–7)

This meant that no representative form of government would be a legitimate government for Naples. By a representative government, Metternich meant a system "which admits an assembly more or less numerous, formed by elections more or less general, deliberating upon questions of state without distinction, and announcing its opinions by means of a parliament and formal address" (November 15, 1820; quoted in Schroeder, 1962:77).

Metternich's view that the Concert needed to take a position on what type of domestic social order was legitimate in Europe, and Metternich's argument that an absolute monarchy was the only legitimate form of domestic social order, were positions adopted by the Concert at the Congress of Troppau. What remained, then, was for questions of domestic social order to be linked to justifications for Concert intervention. This link was made in the Protocol of the Congress of Troppau. The protocol stated:

52

States belonging to the European alliance, which have undergone in their internal structure an alteration brought about by revolt, whose consequences may be dangerous to other states, cease automatically to be members of the alliance. [If such states] cause neighboring states to feel an immediate danger, and if action by the Great Powers can be effective and beneficial, the Great Powers will take steps to bring the disturbed area back into the European system, first of all by friendly representation, and secondly by force if force becomes necessary to this end.

(Quoted in Palmer and Colton, 1971:490; brackets in Palmer and Colton)

The protocol formalized Tsar Alexander's interpretation of the Treaty of Aix-la-Chapelle by stating that the Concert had a right of intervention in European states which experienced a revolution. Because the protocol went on to say that this right of intervention may be invoked if "neighboring states...feel an immediate danger" and because such a danger would be felt as a result of an absolute monarchy being overthrown, the implication of the protocol was that this right of intervention would be invoked in cases of revolutions against absolute monarchies. The protocol further specified that membership in the European community was forfeited by states experiencing revolutions or who had governments which resulted from revolutions. Thus, the Concert secured its community from intrusions by members with illegitimate domestic social orders and established itself as the legitimate community of interpretation concerning matters of social order – both domestic and international.

A Foucauldian analysis

Concert of Europe discourse concerning the Neapolitan Revolution asserted absolute monarchy as the legitimate foundation of European state sovereignty. In so doing, it provided a clear answer to the question, "who is represented?" Concert discourse (and Metternich's in particular) maintained that the Concert was not inventing this foundation; rather, it was merely acting to preserve the existing sovereign foundation whose legitimacy was already beyond question. Revolutionary events in Spain and Naples against legitimate monarchies were evidence of the risks faced by monarchies in Europe generally. And because the European order more generally was built upon absolute monarchies – at least on the continent – the Concert's decision to defend this foundation of order in individual sovereign states and in Europe generally was self-evident.

If, however, one juxtaposes Concert discourse on the Neapolitan Revolution with its discourse concerning the Spanish Revolution, interpretations of *preservation* give way to interpretations of *invention*. One moves from the question "who is represented?" to the Foucauldian question "how is representation possible?" The representation of absolute monarchy as the foundation of sovereign authority was jeapordized by revolutionary movements. Individual states (France and Austria) acted on Concert authority to squash opposition in Spain and Naples to absolute monarchical authority. In so doing, the Concert acted on behalf of European monarchs to punish revolutionaries who had committed crimes against the monarch by committing crimes against the state. The revolutionary bodies of Spain and Naples were *marked* through intervention practices undertaken by the Concert in the name of absolute monarchy. There could be few more emphatic ways of enacting a monarch's declaration that *l'etat c'est moi*. But attempts to punish violence against the stately body and to discredit movements which problematized absolute monarchy discursively *produced* a "true" source of sovereign authority which was neither legitimate nor absolute by Concert standards. By moving onto a Foucauldian consideration of the production of foundational authorities, one can begin to appreciate why conservative institutions such as absolute monarchy and the Concert failed.

In his State Paper of May, 1820, Castlereagh made the British case against Concert intervention in the Spanish Revolution in particular and against a Concert doctrine of intervention more generally. In this document, Castlereagh elaborated on what kind of situation would merit intervention by an individual sovereign state in the internal affairs of another European state, noting that this situation did not exist at the time in Spain.

> The present state of Spain, no doubt, seriously extends the range of political agitation in Europe, but it must nevertheless be admitted that there is no portion of Europe of equal magnitude, in which such a Revolution could have happened, less likely to menace other States, with direct and imminent danger, which has always been regarded, at least in this Country, as alone constituting the Case which would justify external interference. (*BFSP*, vol. 10:72)

Metternich at first embraced Castlereagh's argument, in part as a way to prevent Russian troops from crossing the continent to crush the Spanish rebellion and in part because the revolution seemed unlikely to spread from such a remote corner of Europe as Spain. Furthermore, Metternich wrote to his Ambassador in France that "foreign action has never either arrested or controlled the effects of a revolution," and that domestic affairs must be resolved from within:

> In such a situation [as in Spain] the remedies can only be found in the lands themselves which suffer from the errors and the faults committed by their own governments. Every *material* remedy which a foreigner directs against an internal evil of that kind serves only to augment the evil by giving a very special force to extreme parties.
> (To Vincent, June 15, 1820; quoted in Schroeder, 1962:28 brackets in
> Schroeder)

It is not unheard of for a diplomat to change his mind, and scholarly accounts of Metternich's policy on the Spanish and Neapolitan revolutions point this out, as well as pointing out how Metternich's reconsideration of events was "wise," "cunning," and "strategic."[7] These accounts do not fail to note what a brilliant statesperson Metternich was or how he manipulated his fellow diplomats. For the purposes of my analysis, though, the supposed brilliance and intentionality of Metternich's and others' maneuverings[8] is beside the point. What is of interest is what Metternich's discourse does, the effects it has. How, for example, might Metternich's treatment of the Spanish Revolution as an isolated incident have undermined his discursive strategies pertaining to the Neapolitan Revolution? In particular, did Metternich's discourses concerning each revolution produce different representations of the true location of sovereign authority?

Metternich's discourse on the Spanish Revolution put into question the foundational meanings which his discourse on the Neapolitan Revolution employed. Reading the Spanish case onto the Neapolitan case, one can argue that the meanings of "intervention" and "sovereignty" and the location of sovereign authority in European states in Metternich's discourse were not "discoveries" of deep meaning as Metternich suggested. Rather, they were constructs or inventions that were politically effective in that they marginalized equally plausible alternative interpretations that could have informed Concert policies on the revolutions but politically costly because they contradicted each other.

Metternich's discourse at the beginning of the Spanish Revolution "found" a different basis for determining when intervention was justified and when it was not than it "found" once the Neapolitan Revolution began. As noted earlier, Metternich's discourse accepted the British position that a general right to intervention was not justified every time a European state experienced an internal revolt. For the Concert, revolution – a movement by the subjects or people of a state to dictate to their monarch what form of government their state should adopt – was not in itself reason enough for a foreign state to intervene. As Castlereagh's State Paper argued, a revolution must also be a threat to a neighboring sovereign state for intervention by that sovereign state to be legitimate.

This was a radically different notion than the one announced by the Concert in the Protocol of the Congress of Troppau. Addressing the Neapolitan Revolution but applying equally to all European revolutions, the protocol held that revolution in a European state alone meant that the revolutionary state "ceases automatically" to be a member of the European community. The protocol went on to suggest that if events in the revolutionary state threatened neighboring states, then the Concert could invoke its right of intervention.

While at first the British position and the Concert position appeared to differ only on the question of whether intervention was an individual or a collective right, there was a more important difference. These two positions also differed on the question of what constituted a threat to a neighboring state. In the Concert account, revolution alone automatically constituted a threat to neighboring states. This was not so in the British account. The reason for this difference was that the Concert and British discourses referred to different foundational authorities in making their claims about what constituted a threat to neighboring states.

Castlereagh's State Paper spelled out the British position that a revolution like the Spanish Revolution in which a people rise up to gain a voice in the affairs of their state was not a threat in principle. Castlereagh wrote: "No country having a representative system of Government" could support a collective right to intervene that found its basis in the argument that absolute monarchies must be protected from movements by the people which seek to share in a state's sovereignty" (see Webster, 1958:240).

In the Protocol of the Congress of Troppau, the Concert took the position that any movement from below which challenged monarchical power was illegitimate. As Castlereagh's State Paper anticipated, the Concert position depended upon the argument that absolute monarchy was the only legitimate form of domestic social order. And for this argument to be a "deep truth" that the Concert "discovered" and affirmed, it must be true for all times in all places. It must be true, most importantly, from all perspectives that are supposed to be sovereign. This was the argument that Metternich's discourse on the Neapolitan Revolution made. However, Metternich's discourse on revolutions generally was self-subverting for two reasons.

First, his discourse at the outbreak of the Spanish Revolution, as noted earlier, did not ascribe to this kind of logic. Metternich's discourse did not hold that revolutionaries in Spain must be crushed because they threatened the only legitimate form of domestic social order – absolute monarchy. Rather, Metternich's discourse held that revolutionary events in Spain could be ignored so long as they do not spread to other, more central parts of Europe. Therefore, internal differences could be tolerated so long as they did not implicate other European powers – so long as domestic disputes in one part of Europe did not become threats to the European order more generally.

Second, Metternich's prescriptions for a post-revolutionary government in Naples rejected absolute monarchy as the ideal form of government to be established in Naples. Instead, what was proposed was a government which would be nonthreatening to Austrian and European order. An absolute monarchy in Naples – what Metternich argued for as late as October of 1820 – would leave it solely to the King to decide what form of government Naples should have. Metternich wrote:

> We regard as a matter placed outside our competence [the task] of deciding the future forms of the internal administration of the Kingdom of the Two Sicilies. That right belongs only to the legitimate sovereign ... To wish to impose any form of government whatsoever on the Kingdom, or to forbid any, would be, despite the difference of intentions, to take a course analogous to that of the factions who have imposed their own laws upon it.
> (To Austrian Ambassador to France Vincent, August 12, 1820; quoted in Schroeder, 1962: 63; brackets in Schroeder)

In a document presented at the opening of the Congress of Troppau, Metternich reiterates this position.

> The legitimate power is captive; it is a matter of breaking its chains. It is up to the King to decide what the real interest of his crown and his country demands at the conclusion of this first action. It is for him alone to pronounce it, for him alone to establish it. But to arrive at that legal end, it is necessary that the King be free in his thought and still more that he be supported in his action.
> (Memoire du Cabinet Autrichien, October 23, 1820; quoted in Schroeder, 1962: 64)

Documents authored later concerning the Neapolitan Revolution illustrate that this position was abandoned by Metternich and the Concert. Recall, for example, the document in which Metternich explicitly outlined what form a legitimate post-revolutionary Neapolitan government could take. In this document, Metternich spoke of the need for future institutions in Naples to insure that monarchical sovereignty was not compromised from below, that internal order was secured, and that neighboring sovereign states were not threatened by the new Neapolitan institutions. These prescriptions did not merely reemphasize the legitimacy of absolute monarchy. If they did, then the form of Neapolitan social order would be for the king alone to determine. Rather, what Metternich's discourse did was both (1) reject absolute monarchy on the basis that it could be too dangerous to neighboring states;[9] and (2) shift the location of the sovereign authority from within revolutionary states to the custody of the Concert until such time as the right form of government was reestablished in the revolutionary state. This right form of government would be determined by the Concert.

Metternich's discursive move returns analysis to the content component of the concept of legitimacy. The presumed "norm" of legitimacy held that the Concert as a whole could take a position on what form of domestic social order was legitimate in Europe. As Albrecht-Carrie emphasized, the content component of the doctrine of legitimacy was an intentionally vague concept (Albrecht-Carrie, 1970:20). Rather than specifying the basis and character of the domestic order of sovereign states, all sovereign states within the European system – regardless of their internal composition – presumably enjoyed equal status and privileges. This has to be the case because the Concert was composed of states with different foundations of sovereign authority. For example, Austria and Russia were absolute monarchies – monarchies in which the people or subjects did not have a voice in political affairs – whereas Great Britain was a constitutional monarchy – a monarchy in which the people or subjects were the recognized basis of monarchical power. So long as the social and political order within states did not affect their international status – their international recognition as sovereign states – the Concert could maintain international unity.

Castlereagh's State Paper of May 1820 underscored the contradiction between the two components of legitimacy – acceptance and content. Castlereagh's argument was that the Concert's original charge was to rescue Europe from the military dominance of France and that this charge did not include taking a position in principle on what form of domestic social order was legitimate:

> In this Alliance, as in all other human Arrangements, nothing is more likely to impair, or even to destroy its real utility, than any attempt to push its duties and its obligations beyond the Sphere which its original conception and understood Principles will warrant. – It was in Union for the re-conquest and liberation of a great proportion of the Continent of Europe from the military dominion of France; and

> having subdued the Conqueror, it took the State of Possession, as
> established by the Peace, under the protection of the Alliance. – It
> never was, however, intended as an Union for the Government of the
> World, or for the Superintendence of the Internal Affairs of other
> States. (State Paper, May, 1820, *BFSP*, vol. 10:73–4)

Thus, Castlereagh's discourse challenged the notion that the
Concert had the right to oversee the internal affairs of states.
Moreover, Castlereagh's State Paper argued that Great Britain as a
constitutional monarchy could not support any Concert ruling that
would put in question the legitimacy of constitutional monarchies.

> The principle of one State interfering by force in the internal affairs of
> another in order to enforce obedience to the governing authority, is
> always a question of the greatest possible moral, as well as political,
> delicacy ... It is only important on the present occasion to observe
> that to generalise such a principle and to think of reducing it to a
> system, or to impose it as an obligation, is a scheme utterly impractic-
> able and objectionable ... No country having a representative system
> of government could act upon it, and the sooner such a doctrine shall
> be distinctly abjured as forming in any degree the basis of our
> Alliance the better ... Great Britain has perhaps equal power with any
> other State to oppose herself to a practical and intelligible danger
> capable of being brought home to the national feeling. When the
> territorial Balance of Europe is disturbed, she can interfere with
> effect, but she is the last Government in Europe which can be
> expected or can venture to commit herself on any question of an
> abstract character. (Quoted in Webster, 1958:240)

Castlereagh expressed in this passage the view that Great Britain, a
sovereign state organized as a constitutional monarchy, could not be a
party to any position which would declare that form of political
organization illegitimate. Furthermore, argued Castlereagh, the
Concert need not make a distinction between legitimate and illegitimate forms of domestic order not only because such a distinction
would lead to the exclusion of some members of the Concert but also
because sovereign states threatened by neighboring state's domestic
organizations already had a remedy available to them – namely,
individual acts of intervention.

Notice that Castlereagh's position on the question of a Concert right
of intervention did not hold that any form of domestic social order was
a legitimate basis of a sovereign state. Rather, Castlereagh couched his
argument in such a way as to preserve the foundation of sovereign
authority of his sovereign state. In effect, then, Castlereagh's argument
took a position on legitimate forms of domestic social order against the
Concert as a way of preserving both the legitimacy of the British social

order and the "general and comprehensive system of Public Law" of which the Concert was the formal embodiment. It was not to say that both constitutional and absolute monarchies were legitimate forms of domestic social order; it was to say that the Concert as a political institution could not survive a choice between them. Only continued ambiguity on this question would leave the Concert intact.

What effect did Castlereagh's position have on the Concert "norm" of legitimacy? Castlereagh's interpretation of legitimacy meant that legitimacy as a basic "norm" of the European community only existed as a "norm" if it were not invoked. Specifically, Castlereagh's discourse shows how the two components of the doctrine of legitimacy cancel one another out. If legitimacy meant acceptance as a collective, agreed-upon position taken by the Concert as a whole, then acceptance was only possible so long as the content of the doctrine of legitimacy remained ambiguous. Alternatively, if the content of the doctrine of legitimacy were specified, then acceptance of this content by the Concert as a whole would be impossible because of the different representation of sovereign foundations to which Concert members' political institutions referred.

When the Concert in the Protocol of the Congress of Troppau and other documents specified the content of the doctrine of legitimacy, the Concert as a community ceased to exist. Great Britain became estranged from the Concert because it could not accept the foundational standards which the Concert required to judge legitimate and illegitimate forms of domestic social order. Indeed, the Concert as a community of sovereign states which adhered to a "general and comprehensive system of Public Law in Europe" never existed. The Concert was never more than the formalization of a military alliance against France. Once the abstract principles upon which Concert member's claimed to be a community were articulated, the Concert was exposed as never having been a community at all.

5 WILSON ADMINISTRATION ACTIONS IN THE MEXICAN AND BOLSHEVIK REVOLUTIONS

... the people cannot decide until somebody decides who are the people.

Sir Ivor Jennings[1]

While in the early 1800s the Concert of Europe mobilized its influences to counter the tide of liberalism, by the early 1900s President Woodrow Wilson championed the cause of liberalism as the basis for legitimate government everywhere. Wilson dedicated his administration to making the world safe for democracy (and capitalism), and the principle which would enable liberal-capitalist, democratic governments to flourish around the world was self-determination. The people, Wilson held, must select for themselves their own form of governance, and, accordingly, other peoples must respect this process.

This shift from monarchical sovereignty to popular sovereignty provided a new answer to the question, "who is represented?" The political representation of popular sovereignty (sign) required that the people (signified) be represented as the foundation of a state's sovereign authority. A popularly elected government (signifier) would represent the people. While clarifying issues of political representation, the symbolic representation of the people was far from resolved. Left unanswered were the questions: who are the people and who can represent them politically?

When the Wilson Administration looked abroad with hopes of universalizing the *sign* of representative government based on popular sovereignty and self-determination, it encountered innumerable obstacles, the most disturbing yet most promising of which was revolution. During times of revolution, no clear domestic community or citizenry could be identified, for the citizenry was divided over the very issues that must be settled in order for the principles of popular sovereignty to find practical political expression. In Mexico and the newly forming Soviet Union, distinct political factions claimed to be

61

the legitimate political representatives of their respective peoples. How the people were symbolically represented – how the people were produced as a particular community from which the source of sovereign authority originated – was disputed. The Wilson Administration became involved in the Mexican and Bolshevik revolutions in order to encourage transitions to representative democracy. If successful, these newly democratic nation-states would circulate as signs that the people were the true source of sovereign authority and that their political representation was inevitable.

By elaborating their justifications for becoming involved in these disputes, the Wilson Administration contributed to the symbolic representation (the production) of the Mexican and Russian people. The administration argued that its actions were justified on the basis of aiding the sovereign peoples of Mexico and Russia, even when the acts themselves violated the sovereignty of these very peoples.

The Mexican revolution

When President Wilson assumed office, the Taft government had not yet recognized the government of General Victoriano Huerta. President Taft's Secretary of State Philander Knox regarded Huerta's rebellion against and probable assassination of President Francisco Madero as "a matter of local criminal law and not of international law" (quoted in Callcott, 1977:302). For the Taft Administration, recognition of Huerta's provisional government hinged upon Huerta's willingness to settle United States economic claims against Mexico. Neither these claims nor, consequently, the issue of United States recognition of the Huerta government was settled when the Wilson Administration inherited the situation.

President Wilson approached events somewhat differently than did Taft. Having campaigned against the "dollar diplomacy" of the Taft Administration, President Wilson was not persuaded that United States economic interests should dictate United States' political interests. Of more immediate concern to President Wilson was the issue of what form of government should succeed the provisional government. Where did sovereignty reside in Mexico and who should a government represent as its source of sovereign authority?

Wilson's policy in Mexico appears to be a version of the Roosevelt corollary to the Monroe Doctrine, which holds:

> Chronic wrongdoing, or an impotence which results in a general loosening of the ties of civilized society, may in America, as elsewhere, ultimately require intervention by some civilized nation, and

> in the Western Hemisphere the adherence of the United States to the Monroe Doctrine may force the United States, however reluctantly, in flagrant cases of such wrongdoing or impotence, to the exercise of an international police power.   (Quoted in Greene, 1957: 5)[2]

Wilson insisted his policies embodied something more: "The function of being a policeman in Mexico has not appealed to me, nor does it appeal to our people ... Our duty is higher than that" (quoted in Callcott, 1977: 357).

Frank Cobb, a member of the Wilson administration, expressed his view: "As the Monroe Doctrine was aimed at the Holy Alliance, so the Wilson doctrine is aimed at the professional revolutionists, the corrupting concessionaires and the corrupt dictators of Latin America ... It is a bold and a radical doctrine" (quoted in Callcott, 1977: 316). And in a radical move for the times, Wilson tied together the issues of orderly governance in a sovereign state and prospects for international cooperation.

> The present situation in Mexico is incompatible with fulfillment of international obligations on the part of Mexico, with the civilized development of Mexico herself, and with the maintenance of tolerable political and economic conditions in Central America. It is upon no common occasion, therefore, that the United States offers her counsel and assistance.
> (President's address to Congress, August 27, 1913; quoted in Robinson and West, 1917: 191)

Formal recognition would not be granted to the Huerta government until assurances were made that open and democratic elections would be held to install a popularly elected government, and that President Huerta would not be a candidate in those elections. Although not explicitly stated, it was the hope of the Wilson Administration that such a government would be liberal/democratic/capitalist and would be amicable toward the United States both politically and economically (Link, 1954: 107; and 1979: Chapter 1).

President Wilson did not view these negotiations nor the withholding of United States' recognition from the Huerta government as interference in the affairs of the Mexican people. Throughout Wilson's presidency and in light of the extraordinary "involvement" of the US in Mexican affairs, President Wilson maintained that he never had and indeed never would intervene in the affairs of the Mexican people (Levin, 1968).

The Huerta government had another view of United States' involvement. Huerta's Foreign Minister Gamboa expressed the view that

United States' advisement on Mexican governance threatened the very sovereignty of the Mexican state:

> If even once we were to permit the counsels and advice (let us call them) of the United States of America not only would we...forgo our sovereignty but we would as well compromise for an indefinite future our destinies as a sovereign entity and all the future elections for president would be submitted to the veto of any President of the United States of America.　　　　　(Quoted in Link, 1954:114)

Negotiations were underway between the United States and Mexico on the issue of elections when on October 10, 1913, Huerta arrested and imprisoned 110 members of the Chamber of Deputies, inaugurating a military dictatorship. President Wilson declared that no free or democratic elections could take place in an atmosphere of military rule. The Wilson Administration's immediate policy goal thus was rendered unrealizable. President Wilson responded in his annual message to the Congress:

> Mexico has no government. The attempt to maintain one at the City of Mexico has broken down, and a mere military despotism has been set up which has hardly more than the semblance of national authority ... [A] condition of affairs now exists in Mexico which has made it doubtful whether even the most elementary and fundamental rights either of her own people or of the citizens of other countries resident within her territory can long be successfully safeguarded, and which threatens, if long continued, to imperil the interests of peace, order, and tolerable life in the lands immediately to the south of us.
> (Delivered by Wilson on December 2, 1913; quoted in Robinson and West, 1917:204)

On April 22, 1914, President Wilson ordered the US Marines to occupy Vera Cruz, Mexico. Thinly veiled behind claims to avenge American honor in light of the Mexican refusal to salute the American flag as an apology for imprisoning two US servicemen, the President was quick to admit that the occupation was an attempt to discredit and lead to the political downfall of President Huerta. And President Wilson justified his action with reference to the Mexican people. Commenting on US actions the day following the landing, Wilson said:

> I wish to reiterate with the greatest earnestness the desire and intention of this Government to respect in every possible way the sovereignty and independence of the people of Mexico.
> ... Wherever and whenever the dignity of the United States is flouted, its international rights or the rights of its citizens invaded, or

64

its influence rebuffed where it has the right to attempt to exercise it, this Government must deal with those actually in control. It is now dealing with General Huerta in the territory he now controls. That he does not rightfully control it does not alter the fact that he does control it.

We are dealing, moreover, only with those whom he demands and those who come to his support. With these we must deal. They do not lawfully represent the people of Mexico. In that fact we rejoice, because our quarrel is not with the Mexican people, and we do not desire to dictate their affairs. But we must enforce our rightful demands upon those whom the existing authorities at the place where we act do, for the time being, represent.

(Quoted in *New York Times*, April 24, 1914)

President Wilson's distinction between a government and a people in this context surprised some members of the supposed international community. And indeed this surprise is not unfounded. For it does seem to be ironic that the President of one sovereign state would justify his sending troops into another state on behalf of the sovereign people in that state. Yet to President Wilson, no such paradox existed. How this could be the case depends upon where sovereignty is invested and what intervention means.

For President Wilson, the foundation of any legitimate government was its citizenry. In this sense, Wilson was able to declare the Huerta government illegitimate and once again to tie domestic governance to the issue of international cooperation:

Co-operation is possible only when supported at every turn by the orderly processes of just government based upon law, not upon arbitrary or irregular force. We hold, as I am sure all thoughtful leaders of republican governments everywhere hold, that just government rests always upon the consent of the governed, and that there can be no freedom without order based upon law and upon the public conscience and approval.

(Wilson, March 11, 1913, quoted in Robinson and West, 1917:179)

Furthermore, President Wilson maintained that US involvements in Mexico did not constitute intervention. During 1914 when the Vera Cruz incident was a focus of attention in United States–Mexican relations, the Wilson Administration publicly and privately denied suggestions that US actions constituted interference much less intervention in Mexican affairs. What intervention meant and – in the Wilson Administration's view – where the limits of Mexican sovereignty might be were not seriously entertained. This was the case, it seems, for two reasons.

First, and as has been mentioned, the Wilson Administration's preoccupation was that the source of sovereign authority – the Mexican people – be represented by a Mexican government. Therefore, from Wilson's induction as President until formal US recognition of the Carranza government in 1917, this issue was of primary concern to the administration and overshadowed all others in United States–Mexican relations.

Second, because the source of sovereign authority could not be guaranteed representation – because the Mexican people could not be represented symbolically or politically by a (or this, i.e., Huerta's) Mexican government – the issue of where the limits of their (and thus the state's) authority might be could not yet become an issue. What *was* at issue was if the Mexican state could be treated as sovereign at all.

The questionable sovereignty of the Mexican state was entwined with the notion of intervention. In his denials of United States' intervention in Mexico, the President supported this claim by adding that the United States did and would continue to respect the sovereignty of Mexico. It may be inferred from his statement that Wilson understood intervention to be a violation of sovereignty. Such an understanding of intervention enabled President Wilson to make a connection between the meaning of intervention and the location of sovereignty. He held that the Provisional Government of Mexico as ruled by Huerta was not sovereign because it was not a government of, by, and for the Mexican people. Thus, the Mexican state represented by the Provisional Government was not sovereign. By this logic, then, the US action could not be intervention because it was directed against the Provisional Government – an agent of the state that was not sovereign. If one accepts this logic, then the claim to act on behalf of the sovereign people of Mexico while acting against the Provisional Government did not amount to a contradiction.

One additional point bears mentioning. Wilson Administration denials of intervention in Mexico were based upon this crude understanding of intervention as an invasion of state sovereignty. At this period in United States–Latin American relations, intervention in its practical form referred to policing practices whereby the United States government established itself as the occupying protectorate of a Latin American state, as occurred for example in Haiti and Cuba. But protectorate status for Mexico was never entertained as a US policy option.

Beyond this practical understanding, a more content-specific meaning of the term intervention was not elaborated until some three years later when in 1916 US troops again crossed into Mexican territory. While agreement was never reached between the United States and Mexican parties as to what actions constituted intervention, the existence of debate alone was of importance because it politicized actions and their justifications.

The Pershing Expedition

After the fall of Huerta, the Constitutionalists split into two factions – one led by General Venustiano Carranza and another led by Francisco "Pancho" Villa. Initially, the Wilson Administration supported the Villa faction, believing that Villa could more quickly bring an end to rebellion in Mexico. But when Villa's successes waned, the Wilson Administration backed the Carranza faction instead. Villa avenged himself against the United States by crossing into United States territory and killing US citizens in Columbus, New Mexico, on March 9, 1916. President Wilson responded by sending Brigadier General Pershing into Mexico in pursuit of Villa, insisting that such an act did not violate Mexican sovereignty.

> An adequate force will be sent at once in pursuit of Villa with the single object of capturing him and putting a stop to his forays. This can and will be done in entirely friendly aid of the constituted authorities in Mexico and with scrupulous respect for the sovereignty of that Republic.
>
> (A statement by the President to the press; cited in FRUS,[3] 1916:484)

The Carranza government responded immediately indicating that such action, if taken unilaterally by the United States in the absence of negotiation with and agreement by the Mexican government, would be resented and would very probably lead to war. In a cable dated March 10, 1916, the Carranza government elaborated its terms for possible US pursuit of Villa in Mexican territory. The cable, sent through United States Special Agent Silliman, referred to raids into Mexican territory by Indians resident in US reservations and the precedent established that either government could pursue such raiding parties across the international border. It continues:

> Bearing in mind these precedents and the happy results to both countries yielded by the agreement above referred to, the Government over which the citizen First Chief [General Carranza] presides, desiring to exterminate as soon as possible the horde led by Francisco Villa, who was recently outlawed, and to capture Villa and adequately punish him, applied through you, Mr. Confidential Agent, to the Government of the United States and asked that the Mexican forces be permitted to cross into American territory in pursuit of the aforesaid bandits led by Villa, upon that understanding that, reciprocally, the forces of the United States may cross into Mexican territory,

if the raid effected at Columbus should unfortunately be repeated at any other point on the border.
(Mexican Secretary of Foreign Affairs Acuna to Special Agent Silliman; *FRUS*, 1916:485)

The crucial phrase in this cable is "if the raid effected at Columbus should unfortunately be repeated at any other point on the border." The notion here was that the Carranza government was dealing and would continue to deal with the Columbus incident. Only if these efforts failed and Villa struck in US territory again would the Mexican conditions apply. Until such time, US troops in Mexico would be regarded "as an invasion of national territory" (Carranza to Mr. Arredondo, March 11, 1916; *FRUS*, 1916:486).

Intentionally or unintentionally, the Wilson Administration did not interpret the Carranza government's terms as precluding immediate pursuit of Villa in Mexico prior to another raid in United States territory. Cables exchanged over the next few days express satisfaction by both parties about their mutual agreement. Secretary of State Lansing sent assurances to the Carranza government that the United States "punitive expedition" would alleviate the possibility of intervention.

> In order to remove any apprehension that may exist either in the United States or in Mexico, the President had authorized me to give in his name the public assurance that the military operations now in contemplation by this Government will be scrupulously confined to the object already announced [pursuit of Villa], and that in no circumstances will they be suffered to trench in any degree upon the sovereignty of Mexico or develop into intervention of any kind in the internal affairs of our sister Republic. On the contrary, what is now being done is deliberately intended to preclude the possibility of intervention.
> (Robert Lansing to Mr. Arrendondo, March 13, 1916; *FRUS*, 1916:489).

When the misunderstanding was discovered some nine days later, the Carranza government entered into more specific negotiations with the United States, only to learn that US troops had entered Mexican territory in the absence of either an agreement with or notification to the Mexican government. US troops remained in Mexico (largely because the Mexican government hoped to avoid war with the United States) while negotiations covering their conduct continued.[4] On April 3, 1916, Secretary of State Lansing expressed the Wilson Administration's approval of an agreement outlining the terms under which foreign troops would be permitted on either United States or Mexican soil – so long as the agreement did not pertain to United States troops already in Mexico:

> The Government of the United States, in entering into the reciprocal agreement with the *de facto* Government of Mexico relative to the pursuit of lawless bands across the international boundary by the military forces of the respective Governments, does so on the understanding that the conditions imposed by that agreement are not to be applied to the forces of the United States now in Mexico in pursuit of Villa and his bandits who attacked and burned Columbus, New Mexico, killing a number of American citizens, the said forces having entered Mexico under a previous agreement which arose out of the outrage perpetrated by outlaws at Columbus on March 9th.
> (Lansing to Mr. Arredondo, April 3, 1916; *FRUS*, 1916:507)

The Mexican government responded in a long cable which summarized events up to this point. In addition to other issues, it stated:

> the Government of Mexico...necessarily believed in the supposition that the American Government was fully convinced that the expedition sent forth on Mexican territory in pursuit of Villa is without a foundation because of there existing no previous agreement on the subject which has been the only motive of the discussion until this moment.
>
> Furthermore...the Government of the United States had acted in good faith in sending its expedition into Mexico in pursuit of Villa, in the supposition that the note of March 10 contained a definite agreement; and that the American Government agreed that the expedition should remain on Mexican territory only while the details of the agreement were being concluded.
>
> If now the American Government pretends that the expedition sent against Villa should be considered as an exceptional case, and that it should remain outside of the terms of the agreement, it appears altogether useless to continue discussing the conditions and details of same ...
>
> In consequence of the above ... the Government of Mexico believes that it is advisable, for the present, to suspend all discussions or negotiations relative to this matter, and considering that the expedition sent by the Government of the United States to pursue Villa is without warrant, under the circumstances, because there existed no previous formal or definite understanding, and because this expedition is not fulfilling its object and undoubtedly cannot do so, because the band headed by Villa has already been dispersed, and finally, because there are sufficient Mexican troops to pursue him...it is now time to treat with the Government of the United States upon the subject of the withdrawal of its forces from our territory.
> (Secretary of Foreign Relations C. Aguilar to Secretary of State Lansing, April 12, 1916; *FRUS*, 1916:517)

Thus, subsequent discussion expressed the Mexican government's objective to remove US troops from Mexican territory and the US government's intention to remain in Mexico until Villa was captured by either government. Generals of both armies met on March 24, 1916, in hopes of reaching agreement on these conflicting points. They achieved partial success. While the Mexican government failed to achieve agreement on a definite date for total US troop evacuation from Mexican territory, the US government did agree to begin a gradual withdrawal of troops. Of particular interest is that the US government couched its agreement in terms of the capacity of the Mexican government to control its own territory in the absence of US troops. The joint memorandum of March 24 meeting states:

> The decision of the American Government to continue the gradual withdrawal of the troops of the punitive expedition from Mexico was inspired by the belief that the Mexican Government is now in a position and will omit no effort to prevent the recurrences of invasion of American territory and the completion of the withdrawal of American troops will only be prevented by occurrences arising in Mexico tending to prove that such belief was wrongly founded.
> (*FRUS*, 1916:539)

This statement complemented a statement made by President Wilson to the US Congress in which he justified the Pershing expedition in terms of Mexico's incapacity to meet its international obligation of policing international lawlessness on the part of Villa:

> Our recent pursuit of bandits into Mexican territory was no violation of that principle [not take advantage of small states]. We ventured to enter Mexican territory only because there were no military forces in Mexico that could protect our border from hostile attack and our own people from violence, and we have committed there no single act of hostility or interference ever with the sovereign authority of the Republic of Mexico herself. It was a plain case of the violation of our own sovereignty which could not wait to be vindicated by damages and for which there was no other remedy. The authorities of Mexico were powerless to prevent it.
> (Brackets in original; Address to Congress on September 2, 1916; quoted in Robinson and West, 1917:343–4)

Notice in this passage Wilson's reference to "the sovereign authority of the Republic of Mexico herself." This is another example of Wilson's differentiation between the sovereign people of Mexico and in this case the *de facto* government of Mexico.

The Wilson Administration further maintained that the Pershing expedition did not constitute an act of intervention by the United

States into the affairs of the Mexican people. Of note at this juncture, however, is that the meaning of intervention was not left open as a matter of public, international debate. Rather, the specific implications of the term intervention were a matter of state policy.

In a cable[5] to President Wilson about Villa's attack on Columbus and the subsequent Pershing expedition, Secretary of State Lansing expressed his view that the incident "is simply a state of international war without purpose on our part other than to end the conditions which menace our national peace and the safety of our citizens, and that is *not* intervention with all that word implies" (*FRUS*, 1916:559). The Secretary elaborated that:

> We have long denied any purpose to interfere in the internal affairs of Mexico ... Intervention conveys the idea of such interference.
>
> Intervention, which suggests a definite purpose to "clean up" the country, would bind us to certain accomplishments which circumstances might make extremely difficult or inadvisable, and, on the other hand, it would impose conditions which might be found to be serious restraints upon us as the situation develops.
>
> Intervention also implies that the war would be made primarily in the interest of the Mexican people, while the fact is it would be a war forced on us by the Mexican Government, and, if we term it intervention, we will have considerable difficulty explaining why we had not intervened before but waited until attacked.　(*FRUS*, 1916:558–9)

The Secretary elaborated what he viewed as the differences between intervention and non-intervention in a memorandum to the President.[6]

> To intervene in the affairs of a neighboring independent state means to interfere with its domestic affairs and the exercise of its sovereign rights by its people. ... when I became Secretary of State, I realized that the continued conditions of lawlessness and violence in the northern states of Mexico might at any time compel us to employ force to protect the American border and American citizens against the bands of armed men who were committing degradations in that region, and that, if we were compelled to send troops into Mexico, it could only be construed as intervention between the factions which were striving to obtain control of the government. Without a recognized government we could not cause a state of international war between the United States and Mexico.
>
> In view of the policy of non-intervention and the satisfaction with which it had been received by the Latin American Republics to be forced to adopt a course of intervention although the actual purpose was protection of American rights and territory would have placed the Government in an awkward position.
>
> It was important, therefore, to recognize a government in Mexico

71

as soon as opportunity offered in order to avoid a condition which forced us into the false position of intervention. (*FRUS*, 1916:560).[7]

In agreement with Lansing's use of the term, Wilson publicly took pains to invest the term intervention with precise meaning. He stated:

> By intervention I mean the use of the power of the United States to establish internal order there without the invitation of Mexico and determine the character and method of her political institutions. We have professed to believe that every nation, every people, has the right to order its own institutions as it will, and we must live up to that profession in our actions in absolute good faith.
>
> (In *Ladies Home Journal*, October 1916; quoted in Scott, 1918:408)

The Bolshevik revolution

Events in Russia in March of 1917 reassured Wilson that democratic good was winning out over imperialistic evil on a world scale. The authoritarian regime of Tsar Nicholas II, confronted by labor strikes and bread riots, gave way to a Provisional Government on March 15, 1917.[8] United States Ambassador to Russia Francis pronounced the revolution as "the practical realization of that principle of government which we have championed and advocated, I mean government by consent of the governed" (to Lansing, March 18, 1917, *FRUS*, 1917:1207). The Wilson Administration granted almost immediate recognition to the Provisional Government[9] and, as would prove important later, established formal diplomatic ties with the government, exchanging ambassadors and embassy staff.

In his War Message to the Congress, President Wilson declared:

> Does not every American feel that assurance has been added to our hope for the future peace of the world by the wonderful and heartening things that have been happening within the last few weeks in Russia? Russia was known by those who knew it best to have been always in fact democratic at heart, in all the vital habits of her thought. .. The autocracy that crowned the summit of her political structure, long as it had stood and terrible as was the reality of its power, was not in fact Russian in origin, character, or purpose; and now it has been shaken off and the great, generous Russian people have been added in all their naive majesty and might to the forces that are fighting for freedom in the world, for justice, and for peace.
>
> (Wilson on April 2, 1917 in Baker and Dodd, 1925–1927, vol. 5, pp. 12–13)

As with respect to factions within Mexico during its revolution, the President distinguished between forces of oppression and false representation – in this case the Tsar's government – and the forces of liberty and true national spirit – the liberal forces in Russia, the Russian people as represented by the Provisional Government. Notice that at this early juncture in what was to be the beginning rather than – as many supposed at the time – the end of revolutionary events in Russia, the Wilson Administration participated in symbolically linking the Provisional Government with the Russian people. This was because, in the view of the Wilson Administration, the Provisional Government was the legitimate political representative of the Russian people. For in a liberal-capitalist world order, a liberal-capitalist Russian government must be the natural successor to authoritarian rule.[10]

On November 7, 1917, the liberal path of the Russian Revolution was interrupted when the Bolsheviks ousted the Provisional Government from power. While Wilson Administration officials had been aware of the frailty of the Provisional Government now led by Alexander Kerensky, the United States had never taken the Bolsheviks or their leader V. I. Lenin seriously as a sustainable threat (Gardner, 1976:25). With the Bolsheviks having seized power, the Wilson Administration did not expect them to remain there for long. President Wilson expressed this view to Representative Frank Clark of Florida in a personal letter shortly after the Bolshevik takeover:

> I have not lost faith in the Russian outcome by any means. Russia, like France in the past century, will no doubt have to go through deep waters but she will come out upon firm land on the other side and her great people, for they are a great people, will in my opinion take their proper place in the world.
>
> (Letter dated November 13, 1917; Baker, 1927–1929, vol 7:355)

Notice Wilson's reference to the French Revolution. This seems to suggest that Wilson regarded the Bolshevik rise to power in Russia as but a dark episode in the liberal revolution begun in Russia with the overthrow of the Tsar.[11] The "firm land" upon which a future Russian government would be established was the Russian people. At this early juncture, Wilson viewed the Bolsheviks as an extreme anti-imperialist element that could be brought back in line with the liberal-democratic-capitalist ideals of Kerensky.[12] While Wilson shared the Bolshevik's disdain for traditional imperialists like the Germans, he did not seem to appreciate Lenin's argument that capitalism necessarily leads to imperialism and the implication therein that the United States was an imperialistic power.[13] Nor, at this point, did Wilson pursue rumors of collusion between the Germans and the Bolsheviks. In an address to the American Federation of Labor on November 12, 1917, the President explained:

May I not say that it is amazing to me that any group of persons should be so ill-informed as to supposed, as some groups in Russia apparently suppose, that any reforms planned in the interest of the people can live in the presence of a Germany powerful enough to undermine or overthrow them by intrigue or force? Any body of free men that compounds with the present German Government is compounding for its own destruction. But that is not the whole of the story. Any man in America or anywhere else that supposes that the free industry and enterprise of the world can continue if the Pan-German plan is achieved and German power fastened upon the world is as fatuous as the dreamers in Russia. What I am opposed to is not the feeling of the pacifists, but their stupidity. My heart is with them, but my mind has a contempt for them. I want peace, but I know how to get it, and they do not.
("Address to The American Federation of Labor at Buffalo, NY, November 12, 1917," in Baker and Dodd, 1925–1927, vol. 5: 120–1).

Even as late as early January, 1918, the President continued to speak of Russia's "independent determination of her own political development and national policy" assuring Russia "a sincere welcome into the society of free nations under institutions of her own choosing" (Wilson, "[Fourteen Points] Address Delivered at a Joint Session of the Two Houses of Congress," January 8, 1918; in Baker and Dodd, 1925–1927, vol. 5: 155–62).

By March, however, Wilson's statements indicated that he was moving the administration away from "watchful waiting" for Bolshevik conversion to liberalism to replaying his distinction between the government and the people. His appeal to the Russian people to reject the Brest-Litovsk Treaty without mention of their Bolshevik leaders offers an early glimpse of this distinction.

May I not take advantage of the meeting of the Congress of the Soviets to express the sincere sympathy which the people of the United States feel for the Russian people at this moment when the German power has been thrust in to interrupt and turn back the whole struggle for freedom and substitute the wishes of Germany for the purposes of the people of Russia? ... I beg to assure the people of Russia through the Congress that it will avail itself of every opportunity to secure for Russia once more complete sovereignty and independence in her own affairs and full restoration to her great role in the life of Europe and the modern world.

The whole heart of the people of the United States is with the people of Russia in the attempt to free themselves forever from autocratic government and become the masters of their own life.
(Wilson, "Message to the People of Russia through the Soviet Congress," March 11, 1918, Official bulletin, No. 255, in Baker and Dodd, 1925–1927, vol. 5: 191)

In this passage, Wilson is talking not to the Bolsheviks but directly to the Russian people. As interpreted by Lloyd Gardner, the passage implies that the Russian people's sovereignty must be secured from both the Germans and the Bolsheviks (Gardner, 1976:38).

The hope of wooing Lenin to a liberal-capitalist position was abandoned for a number of reasons. Among them was that Lenin's seizure of power displaced the Provisional Government, the government which the Wilson Administration regarded as the legitimate representative of the Russian people. This unfortunate beginning, from the Wilson Administration's point of view, might have been overlooked had Lenin shown some signs of liberal-democratic conversion. Yet he did just the opposite. When the Constituent Assembly met in January, 1918, Lenin dissolved it because he could not control it.[14] Furthermore, the implications of Lenin's anti-capitalist/anti-imperialist policies were sinking in for Wilson and others in his administration, among them Colonel House.

The most troubling immediate factor for the Wilson Administration was the Bolshevik acceptance of the Brest-Litovsk Treaty. The practical affect of this treaty was to officially remove Bolshevik Russia from World War I, releasing Germany from a two-front war. Symbolically, the Brest-Litovsk Treaty demonstrated to Wilson that for all their anti-imperialistic rhetoric, the Bolsheviks were unwilling to make good on these pronouncements by continuing the war against the Central Powers. Taking these issues together, one scholar noted that "after early 1918 the main drift of Wilson's thought in relation to Leninism would have more to do with finding a liberal-nationalist alternative to Bolshevism than with trying to co-opt the Bolsheviks into a democratic Russian order" (Levin, 1968:71).

Allied Intervention in Siberia

As early as December, 1917, the Entente powers considered some form of intervention in Siberia. Siberia was to be the Allied target for several reasons. The United States was actively involved in a project to develop the Trans-Siberian Railway when the Bolshevik revolution began. The railway was an important supply link in Russia's war effort against Germany. When the Bolsheviks signed the Brest-Litovsk Treaty in March, 1918, securing the railway from a potential takeover by the Germans became an Allied priority.[15] Additionally, Siberia was the region of Russia that, by its sheer distance from Petrograd and Moscow, was the most isolated from Bolshevik rule. Its geographic location allowed the Allies to support anti-Bolshevik movements in

75

Siberia without engaging Bolshevik troops. And a number of anti-Bolshevik movements, however lacking in support and resources, were forming in Siberia. Finally, intervention in Siberia was physically possible while intervention into European Russia was not because of World War I. The Allies could enter Siberia by sea without encountering Central Power resistance.

The issue that had to be addressed prior to any intervention was how to oppose both Bolshevism and German imperialism. This was because any intervention imagined at this time would be intervention by the Allies as a whole and not by any individual state. Allied opposition to German imperialism was justified in that the Allies and the Central Powers were at war. But Russia was a former Allied power who had not sided with the Central Powers but who had negotiated a separate peace with them. Thus, the Allies were not at war with Russia. But if Russian neutrality impaired Allied war aims, then maybe Allied opposition to both Bolshevism and German imperialism could be linked.

President Wilson's liberal internationalist agenda linked these problems ideologically. This was so because liberal internationalism[16] equates two very different political dispositions – imperialism and socialism. Both were seen as repressing the nationalistic spirit of what was to Wilson the most privileged political entity because it was the location of sovereign authority – the people. In other words, both denied the political representation of the people. Fusing Allied opposition to imperialism and socialism into a specific Allied intervention policy in Siberia was a more delicate problem.

One possibility was to pursue theories of collusion between Lenin and Trotsky and the Germans. This view was buttressed by the fraudulent Sisson papers (see Levin, 1968:94 and Gardner, 1976:26). A "Bolsheviks as German agents" approach would mean that to oppose either Germany or the Bolsheviks was to oppose both. The German agent theory was entertained briefly by the Wilson Administration, ultimately to be discounted as too simplistic to explain Lenin's complex policies (see Levin, 1968:93). However, as Francis cabled Secretary of State Lansing shortly after the signing of the Brest-Litovsk Treaty, Lenin and Trotsky "may possibly not have been Germany's agents continuously but if [they] had been [they] could not have played more successfully into Germany's hands" (FRUS, 1918–1919, Russia, 1913–1937, vol 1:384). Even if the Wilson Administration had pursued the German agent theory as a way to link German imperialism and Bolshevism, this position would not have solved Allied intervention policy concerns. For, in linking Germany and the Bolsheviks, how could the Allies be at war with Germany but not at war with the Bolsheviks?

A more credible strategy – because it followed from Wilson Administration policies in Mexico, for example – was to articulate an intervention policy in Siberia based upon claims that the Allies were protecting Russian sovereignty. This was not a difficult case to argue with reference to Germany. But how could the Wilson Administration claim that an Allied intervention in Siberia would protect Russian sovereignty when its aim was in part to counter Bolshevism in the region? Such a claim could be credible depending on where the sovereign authority of Russia was said to reside. As in the Mexican illustration, the sovereign authority of Russia was believed by the Wilson administration to reside in the Russian people. It was the Russian people who were to be represented by a Russian government.

The Wilson Administration concluded that the Allied military intervention in Siberia in no way interfered with Russian political sovereignty by distinguishing between the Allied "military action" which it supported and "military intervention" which it condemned (Acting Secretary of State to Ambassador Morris in Japan, August 3, 1918, *FRUS, 1918–1919, Russia*, 1931–1939, vol. 2:328; Secretary of State to Allied Ambassadors, July 17, 1918, *FRUS, 1918–1919, Russia*, vol. 2:288). By military intervention, the administration meant the unilateral landing of Japanese forces in Siberia not incorporated into a broader Allied program. The Japanese forces ideally would have secured the Trans-Siberian railroad, preventing it from falling under Germany's control. A unilateral Japanese military intervention, supported by France and Italy, was opposed by the United States and Britain. The British hoped that their close ties to Trotsky would result in a Bolshevik invitation to intervene in Siberia (*Colonel House Papers*, 1928:400–7). The United States opposed a unilateral military intervention by Japan for political and military reasons. Politically, they feared – in light of the traditional political and military rivalries and racial prejudices between the Russians and the Japanese – Japanese intervention might consolidate fragmented political groups in Siberia on the side of the Bolsheviks in an effort to oppose a military threat from Japan or – still worse – alienate the Bolsheviks to the extent that the Bolsheviks joined Germany against the Allies in the war. Militarily, the United States distrusted Japanese territorial interests in Asia.[17]

Furthermore, while an invitation to intervene in Siberia would please the United States, an invitation from Trotsky was not acceptable. In a meeting with British intelligence officer William Wiseman about Allied intervention, President Wilson expressed his dissatisfaction with both Japanese intervention and Trotsky's credibility. As summarized by Wiseman, the President spoke of a future Allied Commission that would organize the railroads and food supplies, adding: "If in the meantime we were invited to intervene by any responsible and representative body, we ought to do so. An oral or secret agreement with Trotsky would be no good since he would repudiate it"[18] (Wiseman to Drummond, May 30, 1918, quoted in Levin, 1968:96; see also Lansing to Wilson, *FRUS, Lansing Papers, 1914–20*, 1937, vol. 2:360–1).

While the Allies could not agree as to the benefits and liabilities of unilateral Japanese intervention in Siberia, the Allies did agree that, with the signing of the Brest-Litovsk Treaty on March 4, 1918, and its subsequent ratification by the Soviets, the recreation of an eastern front in the war against Germany would avert pressures on the western front (*Colonel House Papers*, 1928:407). The British saw the restoration of the eastern front as the only assurance that the war could be won by the spring of 1919. If the war persisted past the spring, the British argued, Allied resources would be so drained that an Allied victory could not be guaranteed (British cable, June 17, 1918 in *Colonel House Papers*, 1928:410–12). The Wilson Administration, though sympathetic to the British argument, would not risk facilitating a Bolshevik-German military alliance or subverting their liberal-internationalist principles.

While "nuclei [of] self-governing authorities" in Siberia struggled to establish themselves, circumstances offered the Wilson Administration an excuse to intervene. A number of Czechoslovakian troops making their way eastward along the Trans-Siberian railroad in a roundabout effort to reach the western front came into conflict with Bolshevik officials. The incident escalated into a series of shootouts, with the Czech troops eventually occupying a good portion of the Trans-Siberian railroad. To the Allies, this meant that an anti-German, anti-Bolshevik force, friendly to anti-Bolshevik Russians, had accomplished what a unilateral Japanese intervention might have accomplished. With its goal achieved, a unilateral Japanese intervention had little to offer.

In addition to controlling the railroad, the Czech troops' presence in Siberia gave the Allies added reason to enter Siberia. This was so not only because the Czech troops were engaged in battle with former German and Austrian prisoners of war in Russia who were released and armed but also because, as President Wilson saw it, the Czechs were not only Allies but "the cousins of the Russians" (President Wilson to Secretary of State Lansing, June 17, 1918, *FRUS, Lansing*

Papers, 1914–1920, 1939, vol. 2:363). As the diplomatic liaison officer to the Supreme War Council Frazier expressed his views to the Secretary of State,

> If the Allies are to win the war in 1919 it should be a primary object of their policy to foster and assist the national movement in Russia in order to reform an eastern front or at least to sustain such a vigorous spirit of independence in the occupied territories behind the German lines as will compel Germany to maintain large bodies of troops in the east. Allied intervention at the earliest moment is therefore a necessity if any headway is to be made in organizing that eastern front which is essential, if the Allies are to win the war in 1919 before Germany has concentrated her whole strength once more on the encirclement and domination of Russia. At the present moment intervention as a practical policy is easier than it has ever been.
> (July 2, 1918, *FRUS, 1918–1919, Russia*, vol 2:244)

Failure to intervene immediately, Frazier went on, "would mean the abandonment of the Russian people to the [triumphant] militarism of Germany and the destruction of all hope of the resuscitation of Russia as the liberal ally of the western democracies during the war" (brackets in original; July 2, 1918, *FRUS, 1918–1919, Russia*, vol 2:224–5).

President Wilson agreed that the Czech troops could be the Allies point of entry into Siberia. He wrote to his friend and political advisor Colonel House,

> I have been sweating blood over the question what is right and feasible to do in Russia. It goes to pieces like quicksilver under my touch, but I hope I see and can report some progress presently along the double line of economic assistance and aid to the Czecho-Slovaks.
> (July 8, 1918, quoted in *Colonel House Papers*, 1928:415)

What went "to pieces like quicksilver" under Wilson's touch was a clearly identifiable Russian people.

Wilson's mention of economic assistance referred to a proposal forwarded to the President by House. House suggested a program of basic economic relief in Siberia – the Russian Relief Commission[19] – as part of an intervention plan. House saw economic relief and food production programs as a positive way for the United States to both assist anti-Bolshevik governing authorities in Siberia and establish a foothold in the region. The Russian Relief Commission, according to House, should precede military intervention in the area. The later military intervention could be justified due to the necessity to preserve order in Siberia to ensure the success of the Commission (see *Colonel House Papers*, 1928:409). Secretary of State Lansing agreed with House arguing: "Armed intervention to protect the humanitarian work done by the Commission would be much preferable to armed intervention before this work had been begun" (Lansing to Wilson, *FRUS, Lansing Papers, 1914–20*, 1939, vol. 2:363). In late July, 1918, when the Allied forces landed in Siberia, no economic commission had yet been established, although it was subsequently created.

The United States justified its participation in the joint Allied "military action" as follows:

> As the Government of the United States sees the present circumstances, therefore, military action is admissible in Russia now only to render such protection and help as is possible to the Czecho-Slovaks against the armed Austrian and German prisoners who are attacking them and to steady any efforts at self-government or self-defense in which the Russians themselves may be willing to accept assistance. Whether from Vladivostok or from Murmansk and Archangel, the only present object for which American troops will be employed will be to guard military stores which may subsequently be needed by Russian forces and to render such aid as may be acceptable to the Russians in the organization of their own self-defence.
> (Acting Secretary of State to Ambassador Morris in Japan, August 3, 1918, *FRUS, 1918–1919, Russia*, 1931–1937, vol. 2:328; see also Secretary of State to Allied Ambassadors, July 17, 1918, *FRUS, 1918–1919, Russia*, 1931–1937, vol. 2:288)

A Foucauldian analysis

When we as readers ask "what is represented?" Wilson Administration actions in the Mexican and Bolshevik revolutions reveal to us what meanings of sovereignty, intervention and statehood grounded United States policy during the 1910s. For the Wilson Administration, sovereignty resided in the people. Revolutions by the people for representation in political and social institutions were events that should be applauded by the United States and by the international community. The revolutions of the 1910s, like the French Revolution, were against absolute or totalitarian governments. Notice that, for the Wilson Administration, a government and a people were not identical. If the Wilson Administration had equated governments and peoples, revolutions understood as a contest to capture the political representation of a state between a government and a people would not make sense.

Even though the foundation of sovereign authority resided in the people, according to Wilson, the people may at times lack the capacity to organize themselves into a sovereign state. Revolutions were an instance of such times. Liberal revolutions were moments in history when a people of a state attempted to assert themselves as the true source of sovereign authority within the state (something that was true no matter how a state was organized) and put in place a government which represented them. Before this process was successfully completed, however, a state was not sovereign. It would still be ruled by a government that did not embody the sovereignty of the state because it did not represent the people of the state. Thus, it was possible, by Wilson's account, for a state to be a state but for it not to be sovereign. For a state to be sovereign, it must find the origin of its sovereign authority in its people and represent their sovereign authority in the government.

Intervention for the Wilson Administration was a violation of the sovereignty of a state. Because the sovereign authority of a state was located in the people of a state – in the Mexican and Russian people – then intervention was an act which in some way repressed the sovereign authority of the people. By this account, acts of assistance performed by one sovereign state on behalf of the people of another sovereign state were not acts of intervention. Therefore, US actions in the Mexican and Bolshevik revolutions were not regarded as intervention practices.

How were these representations possible? How, in particular, did intervention justifications participate in producing the Mexican and Russian people as the locations of sovereign authority? And why was it so important to the Wilson Administration to claim that its activities in the Mexican and Bolshevik revolutions were not interventions? To analyze the production of meanings in Wilson Administration discourse, one must turn to Wilson's notion of self-determination. For the principles of self-determination to take practical political form, three criteria must be met. First, a "self" – in this case a domestic political citizenry – must be produced and distinguished from others not included in this population (foreigners and/or non-citizens). In other words, whose views count when determining the political character of the state must *already* be determined. This is important because, as the principle holds, it is a domestic citizenry which must select its own form of governance. Without a domestic citizenry, no such determination can take place.

Second, in order to have a domestic population a clear boundary must exist between the domestic and international spheres. For without such a demarcation, it would be impossible to decide who is included and who is excluded from any particular citizenry.

Third, once identified, a citizenry must be invested with sovereign authority. As it pertains to self-determination, sovereign authority must minimally be exercised to decide what form of governance will prevail in a state. And investing a citizenry of a state with sovereignty implies that a citizenry has the capacity to decide such issues which arise in and pertain to its state.

A corollary to the principle of self-determination which appears in Wilson's discourse is a doctrine of non-intervention. If self-determination maintains that domestic political considerations are solely the affairs of a domestic citizenry, then non-intervention affirms each state's respect for and non-interference in every other state's domestic affairs. Had the Wilson administration claimed to intervene in Mexico and Russia, it would have violated its own doctrine of self-determination.

In the final analysis, self-determination – and all those criteria required to make this principle politically effective – hinges upon narrowing the scope of investigation about "the people." It is tolerable – even encouraged – in this line of thought to ask a number of questions: Who are the people? What is the "true" character of the people? Which political faction or ideology "truly" represents the people? Such questions are allowed because they assume that there is a "real," "true," and stable identity to the people. This identity may be repressed or concealed. It may be underdeveloped or only projected. But what is assumed in each of these questions is that the identity of the people is ultimately decidable and that it can and should be represented.

Posing such questions limits analysis of the people because it disallows questions which do not begin from the assumption that the people do in fact have some true identity. Not grounded in such an assumption, questions about the formation of the people's identity threaten to disrupt the logic of self-determination. If, for example, it is asked *how* the people are constituted as a sovereign identity, then it becomes possible to think of the people as constituted in various ways, no particular one the necessary outcome in history. And if the people can be constituted in any number of ways, then the concept of self-determination can be seen as participating in their constitution rather than as standing for a morally just, apolitical prescription for governance. Once such a thought is allowed, the whole political position of self-determination crumbles.

In this respect, Wilson's foreign policy can be interpreted as firmly devoted not just to the principle of self-determination but also to silencing the very questions that self-determination must not allow to be asked: How is the identity of the people decided? How are the people produced so they can be represented? This was a particularly

difficult task during Wilson's presidency because revolutionary movements in Latin America and Russia were destabilizing their respective
domestic societies. The convenient practice of pointing to a government (signifier) as the representative of a people (signified) often was
not an option because governments were falling and populations were
dividing into opposing political factions. The capacity of the people to
invest a particular government with sovereign authority was at the
very least disrupted. What once appeared to be coherent identities
bound into domestic political communities were dissolving and refor-
ming. In such locales as Mexico and Russia, the identity of the people
was in question.

Wilson's challenge became one of deferring this very question
because the effectiveness of his foreign policy expressed in the principle of self-determination demanded it. Wilson could acknowledge
political unrest in Mexico and Russia interpreted as crises of political
representation. Coming down firmly on the side of the people, Wilson
argued that the people's authorization of a particular state government to serve as its domestic and international agent was repealed. Yet
Wilson could not go beyond this to admit that these crises of representation also were symbolic. Wilson could not recognize that the sovereign authority of the state – the very definition of the people – was also
in crisis. These revolutions were not only battles over which political
faction rightly ought to hold sovereign authority. They were also
battles over how that source of sovereign authority ought to be
molded. To recognize this aspect of the Mexican and Russian revolutions would invalidate Wilson's principle of self-determination.
Therefore, the question of identity formation had to be suppressed at
the very moment when events in Mexico and Russia brought this
question to the fore.

Needless to say, this was no easy task. Nor was it necessarily a
conscious task for the Wilson Administration. How this dilemma was
worked out in Wilson Administration discourse was by preventing it
from ever becoming a dilemma. This was done by focusing on the
question, who is the rightful representative of the people? For Wilson,
the character of the people was "decided-ly" liberal-capitalist democratic. Wilson envisioned two opposing forces at play in history –
democracy which was associated with liberal-capitalist regimes and
totalitarianism which was associated with either "traditional imperialist" regimes (for example, Germany) or with communist and socialist
regimes. Democracy represented "the people"; totalitarianism suppressed "the people." While Wilson never doubted that democracy
would win out in the end, he believed that democratic states must

83

assist and advise not-yet-democratic states in their struggle for democracy. And, not surprisingly, Wilson "discovered" emerging liberal-capitalist democracies in the most unlikely places. Wilson "discovered" them in both the Mexican people who were struggling against authoritarian oppression and in the Russian people who were opposing first an authoritarian Tsar and then the Bolsheviks.

Writing the Mexican people

Turning first to the Mexican Revolution, the strategy of writing or producing the people is illustrated in the US discourse on intervention. Recall Secretary of State Lansing's cable to the President on the Pershing expedition. In this cable, Lansing outlined three criteria which express an act of intervention – interference in the internal affairs of a sovereign state, an effort on behalf of the interfering state to "clean up" the target state, and a justification of the interference as an act undertaken on behalf of the sovereign people in the target state (FRUS, 1916:560). While Lansing's cable is addressed to the Pershing expedition, it is interesting to read it back onto the US occupation of Vera Cruz in 1914 and analyze how the assumptions upon which Lansing's definition rest participate in crafting a very specific form of the Mexican people.

The US action at Verz Cruz could be termed interference because President Wilson made it no secret that the occupation of Vera Cruz was undertaken in the hope of leading to General Huerta's political downfall. Also, the occupation was intended to "clean up" Mexico, at least politically. President Wilson aspired to put in place a Mexican government that would be representative not of a military dictator or of one faction of the Mexican people, but of the Mexican people as a whole. While Wilson's special agent in Mexico Lind commented that the Mexicans politically seemed "more like children than like men" (quoted in Callcott, 1977:353), the President had high aspirations for the Mexican people. One foreign diplomat at the time summed up his impression of Wilson's policy toward Mexico saying that Wilson "propose[d] to teach the South American Republics to elect good men."[20] Furthermore, President Wilson was fond of saying that "when properly directed, there is no people not fitted for self-government" (quoted in Callcott, 1977:357).

As for the basis of this action, the Vera Cruz occupation was justified with reference to the sovereign people of Mexico. The occupation was not undertaken in the name of just any Mexican people, but in the name of a Mexican people understood to be like the people of the

United States. Required in such an understanding was the identifica-
tion of the Mexican people in the image of the people of the United
States, albeit at some earlier moment in their "political development."
In this respect, Lansing's argument was consistent with earlier state-
ments by Wilson. In his book, *Constitutional Government in the United
States*, Wilson wrote:

> Government may be said to have passed, roughly speaking, through
> four stages and forms of development: a first stage in which the
> government was master, the people veritable subjects; a second in
> which the government, ceasing to be master by virtue of sheer force
> and unquestioned authority, remained master by virtue of its insight
> and sagacity, its readiness and firmness to lead; a third in which both
> sorts of mastery failed it and it found itself face to face with leaders of
> the people who were bent upon controlling it, a period of deep
> agitation and full of the signs of change; and a fourth in which the
> leaders of the people themselves became the government, and the
> development was complete. (1908:28)

According to this logic, Mexico was in the third stage – a stage in
which the Mexican people were finding their own voice in matters of
governance but had not yet developed the capacity to rule the state.
The Mexican people were struggling to become politically developed.
Political development – when it was achieved – could easily be recognized, according to Wilson. For in another passage of this work, Wilson
describes political development.

> But the end, whether it comes soon or late, is quite certain to be
> always the same. In one nation in one form, in another in another, but
> wherever conviction is awakened and serious purpose results from it,
> this at last happens: that the people's leaders will themselves take
> control of the government as they have done in England, in Switzer-
> land, in America, in France, in Scandinavia, in Italy, and as they will
> yet do in every country whose polity fulfills the promise of modern
> time. (1908:38)

He continues: "When the fourth and final stage of constitutional
development is reached ... one or other of two forms of government
may result: the parliamentary English form or the American form"
(1908:40).

The telos of political development, according to Wilson, is one or
another form of liberal democracy. The French Revolution was an
early attempt to move from the third to the fourth stage of political
development. Wilson's analogies between the French Revolution and
the Mexican Revolution suggest that the Mexican Revolution was
another such attempt. And the United States – the reproducible sign of

85

institutionalized democracy – expressed the end product of such struggles.

President Wilson told one reporter at the time of the US occupation of Vera Cruz:

> What we desire to do, and what we shall do, is to show our neighbors to the south of us that their interests are identical with our interests; that we have no plans or any thoughts of our own exaltation, but have in view only the peace and prosperity of the people in our hemisphere.   (Quoted in Scott, 1918:391).

Making a claim that the interests of the people of the United States and of Mexico are identical is only possible if the signs of democracy – a citizenry (signified) and a representative government (signifier) – can be produced, exchanged, and reproduced in very different locales.

Writing the Russian people

Wilson's strategy of writing or producing the people was even more apparent during the Bolshevik revolution. This was so because a well-articulated alternative "Russian man" was in circulation in the discourse of the Bolsheviks. This "Russian man" was a proletarian worker or peasant involved in the overthrow of bourgeois institutions. Because Wilson's strategy was to support the "Russian people" and oppose Bolshevism, Wilson's discourse on revolutionary events in Russia had to both construct a "Russian people" that the Wilson Administration could support while simultaneously undercutting the credibility of any alternative constructions of "Russian man," especially the one forwarded by the Bolsheviks.

The first strategy employed in Wilson Administration discourse was to differentiate between the authentic Russian people and the Bolsheviks. A cable from Secretary of State Lansing to the President makes this argument. To the administration, according to Lansing, "the Russian people" were not represented by or identical to the Bolsheviks. This was because, in part, the Bolsheviks claimed to represent "a class and not ... all classes of society, a class which does not have property but hopes to obtain a share by process of government rather than by individual enterprise" (January 2, 1918, *FRUS, 1914–1920, Lansing Papers*, 1939, vol. 2:346). Furthermore, Lansing questioned the Bolshevik's authority to rule.

> it might properly be asked by what authority the Bolsheviks assume the right to speak for the Russian people. They seized the Government at Petrograd by force, they broke up opposition in the army by

disorganizing it, they prevented the meeting of the Constituent Assembly chosen by the people because they could not control it, they have seized the property of the nation and confiscated private property, they have failed to preserve public order and human life, they have acted arbitrarily without pretense of legality, in fact, they have set up over a portion of Russia a despotic oligarchy as menacing to liberty as any absolute monarchy on earth, and this they maintain by force and not by the will of the people, which they prevent from expression.   (*FRUS, 1914–1920, Lansing Papers*, 1939, vol. 2: 348)

United States Ambassador to Great Britain Page reported to the Secretary of State that Great Britain held a similar view of who the Russian people were. He cabled the Secretary: "I discover a growing conviction [on the part of the British] that the Bolshevik regime will soon end and that southern Russia will come forward as the real Russia" (*FRUS, 1918–1919, Russia*, 1931–1937, vol. 2: 33).

Satisfying themselves as to who "the Russian people" were *not*, Wilson Administration officials demonstrated a profound respect for the rights of the Russian people while they projected onto the Russian people a character in their own image.[21]

the Government of the United States is convinced that the spirit of democracy continues to dominate the entire Russian nation. With that spirit the United States feels a profound sympathy and believes in the ultimate effect of its cohesive power upon the Russian people as a whole.

The determination of an agency to exercise the sovereign power of the nation belongs wholly and solely to the Russian people. As to that they ought to be supreme.

The United States has only the kindliest feelings for Russia. Its policy as to recognition or non-recognition of a government at the present time is founded on the principle that the Russian people are sovereign and have the right to determine their own domestic organization without interference or influence by other nations. Its desire to aid the people of Russia rests solely upon the fraternal spirit which it possesses for a great democracy which has endured so much in its struggle against autocracy both within and without its borders. (Draft statement to be issued by Secretary of State Lansing, January 10, 1918, *FRUS, 1914–1920, Lansing Papers*, 1939, vol. 2: 350–1)

Though not stated explicitly, these passages made several assumptions about the Russian people. The Russian people were characterized by their rights and not by any class affiliation. They had the same goals as the peoples of the Allied nations, namely to oppose autocracy and replace it with democracy. And finally, the Russian people could succeed in this struggle if they organized themselves along the international principles of nationalism and sovereignty.

For Wilson Administration officials, the urgency of abating Bolshevik attempts to foundationalize an alternative class-based "Russian people" was not a rhetorical exercise without consequences. Lansing's cable, while it betrays an elitist style which is prejudicial to the working class, alerted the President to what was at stake in Russia – the sanctity of the liberal individual, the principle of sovereignty to which nation-states hold, and the social and political international order. Reacting to Bolshevik suggestions that colonized peoples were wrongly suppressed by imperialist nations and had the right to organize themselves in spite of their incorporation in existing states, Lansing began:

> The suggestions of the Bolsheviks in regard to Ireland, India, and other countries which have been and are integral parts of recognized powers are in my opinion utterly untenable if it is desirable to preserve the present concept of sovereign states in international relations. However justified may be the principle of local self-government, the necessities of preserving an orderly world require that there should be a national authority with sovereign rights to defend and control the communities within the national boundaries.
>
> It is apparent, as I said at the outset, that the Bolsheviks are appealing in this address to a particular class of society, which they seek to arouse against the present order of things, enticing them with the possible abolition of the institution of private property and the possible control by that class of accumulated wealth and of its distribution. The document is an appeal to the proletariat of all countries, to the ignorant and mentally deficient, who by their numbers are urged to become masters. Here seems to me to lie a very real danger in view of the present social unrest throughout the world.
>
> Of course the enforcement of the will of the ignorant, indifferent to all save their own pleasures, would be the worst form of despotism, especially as that class has always been controlled by violent and radical leaders. It would be a species of class-despot, which would have far less regard for private rights than an individual despot. This seems to be the present social program of the Bolsheviks, and they appear to be putting it into operation in Russia. It is essentially anarchistic rather than socialistic in character and will, wherever adopted, break down every semblance of social order and public authority.
> (Lansing to the President; *FRUS, 1914–1920, Lansing Papers*, 1939, vol. 2: 347–8).

The Bolshevik strategy of reinscribing the people was a radical move in the traditional sense of the term radical. This strategy went to the root of the international system – the people organized along nationalistic principles – and reinvented the people by organizing them along class lines. The result was to challenge every institution and principle that the Wilson administration stood for – liberal individuals, the nation-state, sovereignty, and a liberal-capitalist international order. Unable to relinquish the necessity of these institutions and principles as the only acceptable forms of social and political life, Lansing concluded that Bolshevism would result in at best class despotism and at worst anarchy.

Bolshevism, with its alternative construction of the people, jeopardized Wilsonian goals of universalizing equivalent democratic images. It is not much of a stretch to go from Lansing's account of Bolshevism and its implications to the position that the Russian people's sovereignty must be safeguarded against Bolshevism. However, such a position was easier to maintain when a non-Bolshevik, alternative Russian people could be translated from vague rhetorical references into a concrete opposition. President Wilson recognized the value of "discovering" a liberal opposition to Bolshevism among the numerous self-governing authorities in Siberia. The President expressed this notion to Secretary of State Lansing:

> I would very much value a memorandum containing *all* that we know about the several *nuclei* of self-governing authority that seem to be springing up in Siberia. It would afford me a great deal of satisfaction to get behind the most nearly representative of them if it can indeed draw leadership and control to itself.
> (*FRUS, 1914–1920, Lansing Papers*, 1939, vol. 2: 360)

Supporting a "nuclei of self-governing authority" in Siberia would resolve a number of issues for the Wilson administration. If a self-governing authority could be found, it would make tangible the alternative Russian people of whom the administration so often spoke. As noted earlier, Wilson Administration officials could point to former Provisional Government representatives as the Russian people and refer to the ousting of the Tsar as the Russian Revolution. But the Provisional Government had no governing authority within Russia since the Bolshevik revolution. To find a Russian people engaged in political self-determination in Russia would give the Wilson Administration an ideological and territorial foothold in Russia.

The existence of a self-governing authority in Siberia also meant that the semantic play used by the Wilson Administration to distinguish between the Bolsheviks and the Russian people could be simplified. US backing of an organized, self-governing alternative to the Bolsheviks expressed in practice the US position as to who the Russian people were and who they were not.

In terms of the US intervention policy, the existence of a self-governing authority was invaluable. Such a government's opposition to both German imperialism and Bolshevism joined together the two ideological foes the Wilson Administration hoped to oppose through an intervention policy. Furthermore, it did so in a positive way. For, given a US-backed, anti-imperialist, anti-Bolshevik government, the United States could in part justify its intervention policy on the basis of protecting the sovereign authority of this infant government. Thus, what otherwise may have been seen as an oppositional motive could be regarded as a morally justified, "disinterested" attempt toward furthering self-determination in Siberia. The State Department emphasized the disinterestedness of the US government in Russian political affairs and the US respect for Russian sovereignty in a cable circulated to Allied Ambassadors justifying Allied intervention in Siberia.

> In taking this action the Government of the United States wished to announce to the people of Russia in the most public and solemn manner that it contemplates no interference with the political sovereignty of Russia, no intervention in her internal affairs – not even in the local affairs of the limited areas which her military force may be obliged to occupy – and no impairment of her territorial integrity, either now or hereafter, but that what we are about to do has as its single and only object the rendering of such aid as shall be acceptable to the Russian people themselves in their endeavors to regain control of their own affairs, their own territory, and their own destiny.
> (Acting Secretary of State to Ambassador Morris in Japan, August 3, 1918, FRUS, 1918–1919, Russia, 1931–1937, vol. 2:329; see also Secretary of State to Allied Ambassadors, July 17, 1918, FRUS, 1918–1919, Russia, 1931–1937, vol. 2:288–9)

The US claim to non-interference, although *prima facia* counter-intuitive, was not a surprising Wilson Administration claim and made sense if one keeps two points in mind. First, as Levin correctly points out,

> Wilsonian non-interference in the internal politics of Siberia really amounted to a tendency to see all non-Bolshevik and pro-Allied elements as an undifferentiated mass known as "Russia" and a refusal to interfere in the disputes among the rival claimants of anti-Bolshevik and anti-German authority.   (Levin, 1968:110).

This position is supported by the "Proclamation by the Commanders of Allied and Associated Forces at Vladivostok" which attests to the Allies "sympathetic friendship for the Russian people without reference to any political faction or party" (see FRUS, 1918–1919, Russia, 1931–1937, vol. 2:271).

Second, the Wilson Administration concluded that the Allied military action in Siberia in no way interfered with Russian political sovereignty by distinguishing between the Allied "military action" (joint Allied intervention) which it supported and "military intervention" (unilateral Japanese intervention) which it condemned (Acting Secretary of State to Ambassador Morris in Japan, August 3, 1918, *FRUS, 1918–1919, Russia*, 1931–1937, vol. 2:328; Secretary of State to Allied Ambassadors, July 17, 1918, *FRUS, 1918–1919, Russia*, 1931–1937, vol. 2:288).

Thanks to these discursive strategies, the Wilson Administration could claim both that Allied actions in Russia were not intervention and that these actions were undertaken on behalf of the Russian people.

Overall, the Wilson administration policy of self-determination should be interpreted not just as a foreign policy which set out the ideals and goals of that administration and which offered clues as to what sovereignty and intervention meant and where the foundation of sovereign authority resided. Rather, self-determination should be regarded as a political strategy which, through Wilson Administration discourse, worked to silence or defer questions about how "selves" or "identities" were produced by directing analysis toward such questions as: "who were the 'real,' 'true,' Mexican and Russian people?"

By shifting one's interpretive focus from assumptions of decidability and questions about recovery to assumptions of undecidability and questions about production, one politicizes representations. It becomes possible to investigate how decisions about what sovereignty and intervention mean participate in producing and stabilizing representations of the people.

6 UNITED STATES INVASIONS OF GRENADA AND PANAMA

> ... it seems to me people ought to recognize where this request came from...
> Secretary of State George Shultz,
> regarding the Organization of Eastern Caribbean States
> request for US military assistance in Grenada[1]

United States intervention discourse since the Wilson era has made reference to a similar set of claims. No matter where US military action takes place, the US maintains that its action does not constitute "intervention" nor violate the sovereignty of the target state because a discursive distinction has been drawn between a repressive government with no legitimate claim to sovereign authority and the people of the target state who are sovereign.

When confronted with the meanings of sovereignty, intervention, and the people circulating in Reagan–Bush Administration discourse concerning Grenada and Panama, it is no simple proposition to *trace* these meanings back to the Wilson Administration. While recalling all the significant themes of the Wilson Administration – self-determination, democracy, anti–autocracy – the Reagan–Bush Administration discourse encounters difficulties in locating the origins of these themes and their meanings. As during the Wilson era, the foundation of sovereign authority remains the people. However, an answer to the question "who are the people?" cannot be found until one first answers another question, "which international or region community is represented as the center of judgment about who the sovereign Grenadian and Panamanian people are?"

Reagan Administration discourse represents the Organization of Eastern Caribbean States (OECS) – a small regional organization – as the community of judgment about foundational meanings like sovereignty, intervention, and the people. Bush Administration discourse on the Panama invasion is interwoven with Bush Administration discourse on the War on Drugs. I argue that this move transforms the Panama invasion from a foreign policy to a domestic policy concern. Therefore, the community of judgment about foundational meanings is the American people.

The US invasion of Grenada

On October 25, 1983, President Ronald Reagan announced to the American public: "the United States received an urgent, formal request from the five member nations of the Organization of Eastern Caribbean States to assist in a joint effort to restore order and democracy to the island of Grenada" (October 25, 1983; *Public Papers: Ronald Reagan 1983*, 1,505). The OECS states, joined by Barbados, Jamaica, and the United States, engaged in a joint military operation in Grenada. The President justified US participation in this military operation on three grounds – "to protect innocent lives, including up to 1,000 Americans ... to forestall further chaos ... and to assist in the restoration of conditions of law and order and of governmental institutions to the island of Grenada" (October 25, 1983; *Public Papers: Ronald Reagan 1983*, 1,505).

While the protection of American lives has long been a justification for US intervention, forestalling chaos and restoring order echo Wilson era intervention justifications. Indeed, it is the lack of orderly governance in a target state which enables a military action in that state by another state presumably without impinging upon the sovereignty of the target state. This was the Wilson Administration's explanation for why its military activities in the Bolshevik and Mexican revolutions did not constitute violations of the sovereignty of Russia or Mexico and thus were not acts of intervention. The OECS's request for US military assistance noted "the current anarchic conditions, the serious violations of human rights and bloodshed that have occurred and the consequent unprecedented threat to the peace and security of the region created by the vacuum of authority in Grenada".

(Text of OECS Request for Assistance; *American Foreign Policy Current Documents 1983*, 1,397).

The Reagan Administration emphasized this lack of a stable government in Grenada as part of its justification of a military operation. Asked if the military action in Grenada constituted a violation of Grenada's sovereignty, Secretary of State George Shultz based his rejection of this implication on the lack of orderly governance in Grenada:

> There is a vacuum of governmental responsibility. The only genuine evidence of governmental authority being a shoot-on-sight curfew. And so, in the light of that and in the light of the affinity that the

93

other [OECS] states feel together, they felt that they had to protect their peace and their security by taking this action, and in doing so would help reconstitute legitimate government in Grenada.

(Institute of Caribbean Studies, 1984:22).[2]

As Shultz's argument indicates, there is a tendency in the discourse surrounding the Grenada invasion to view the Eastern Caribbean as one region. Prime Minister Eugenia Charles of Dominica, the Chairperson of the OECS, helped to promote this view which has important implications for another Wilsonian theme – self-determination.

In the following passage, Prime Minister Charles reinscribes the notion of self-determination from a national to a regional concept:

> I think we were all horrified at the events that took place recently in Grenada.
>
> We, as part of the Organisation of Eastern Caribbean States, realising that we are, of course, one region, we belong to each, are kith and kin. We all have members of our states living in Grenada.
>
> We are very concerned that this event should take place again.
>
> It is true that we have managed to live with the [Bishop] regime since March '79. And we felt quite clearly and we had good reason to believe that the Bishop regime was seeing it our way and was on the way to have elections. And we think this is the reason why himself and his cabinet were destroyed.
>
> Because he realised that the pressure we put on him to have elections was worthwhile was right. And he began to see that democratic institutions must be put in place in any of these small countries.
>
> It is even more important in a small island state, poor island state, to have the democratic institutions. And this we've had for a long time, and we've continued it and we wish to continue it. Grenada was an aberration in this respect.
>
> But that these men, who had for all these years accepted the Bishop regime should then...decide to destroy the persons whom they had accepted as their leaders for so long, made us realise that *this sort of assassination must not be allowed to continue in our country.*
>
> It means that *our people* there are not safe. It means that Grenadians had never been given the chance to choose for themselves the country that they want. And, therefore, it is necessary for us to see to it that they have the opportunity to do so.
>
> (My italics; Institute of Caribbean Studies, 1984:32).

Regional affiliation blurs the distinction between peoples of different sovereign states. While having initially inscribed "we" as members of the OECS, it is unclear at points whether Prime Minister Charles is referring to all Eastern Caribbean peoples generally or only to non-Grenadians Eastern Caribbeans when she speaks of "our people" in "our country." This inability to determine who the "we" is puts the sovereignty of Grenada into question, more so than would a clearly encoded regional "we" because oscillating between two "we's" suggests that neither "we" is privileged. It suggests that Grenada is part of the Eastern Caribbean community, even though it is significantly different in political form. Furthermore, the oscillation between the two "we's" allows the OECS to occupy two positions at once. One "we" allows the OECS to be so closely associated with Grenada that Grenadian self-determination is legitimately an OECS issue.[3] Reagan Administration discourse made constant reference to this "we," noting that:

> neighbors have a clear, ongoing responsibility to act in ways consistent with each other's legitimate security concerns. ... we have already learned what may be the underlying lesson of the collective response to the Grenada crisis: the best source of knowledge about an area is the people of that area – those most directly concerned with what is happening in their own neighborhood.
> The Caribbean leaders faithfully *reflected* the feelings, the concerns, and hopes of the Grenadian people...
> (My italics; Address by Deputy Secretary of State Dam, November 4, 1983; *American Foreign Policy Current Documents 1983*, 1,424–5)

And as Secretary of State Shultz stressed, "The Caribbean is in our neighborhood, too, so we have a very legitimate affinity for those people" (Transcript of a Press Conference, October 25, 1983; *American Foreign Policy Current Documents 1983*, 1,405).

From this interpretive position which sees the Eastern Caribbean as one region, an OECS request for regional assistance cannot be read as an act of intervention. Prime Minister Charles makes this point in a joint news conference with President Reagan.

> Q. Mr. President, do you think that the United States has the right to invade another country to change its government?
> *The Prime Minister.* But I don't think its an invasion – if I may answer that question.
> Q. What is it?
> *The Prime Minister.* This is a question of our asking for support. We are one region. Grenada is part and parcel of us, an organization –
> Q. But you're sovereign nations, are you not?
> *The Prime Minister.* – and we don't have the capacity, ourselves, to see to it that Grenadians get the freedom that they're required to have to choose their own government.
> (*Public Papers: Ronald Reagan, 1983*, vol. 2: 1,507)

Prime Minister Charles discursively erases the sovereign territorial boundary surrounding Grenada and replaces state sovereignty with regional sovereignty. This move dissociates the request for regional assistance from a violation of state sovereignty.

The other "we" enables the OECS to reflect on regional issues from a concerned but detached position. This second position serves two purposes. First, it makes it possible for the OECS to argue that events in Grenada constitute an external security threat, thus making it possible to invoke Article 8 of the OECS treaty to justify military action.[4] Second, this "we" allows the OECS to serve as the international community of judgment in the US discourse on the Grenada invasion. Prime Minister Charles claims this interpretive space when she answers the question addressed to President Reagan. Because it is an international community (the OECS) rather than the Reagan Administration which reinforces some distinctions (invasion vs. assistance) and blurs others (regional boundaries vs. state boundaries), the Grenada invasion is a matter of US foreign policy.

The final "we" of concern in the Grenada invasion discourse is the "we" which refers to the Grenadian people and which serves as the foundation of sovereign authority in Grenada. This "we" appears in OECS discourse as "part and parcel" and "kith and kin" of the Eastern Caribbean peoples. Therefore, this "we" occasionally is voiced through the OECS. Another compatible inscription of the Grenadian people is that offered by the Reagan Administration. In Wilsonian style, the Grenadian people appear as would-be democrats, if only they were given the chance to express their true political beliefs. Following Wilson's lead, this "we" is inscribed by opposing it to known detractors of the democratic process – authoritarians and communists. Again and again Reagan Administration officials mined the "external enemies handbook" under the entries of "Cuban," "Soviet," "Sandinistas," "Afghanistan invasion," and "terrorists." It seems that all US foes were or were about to be amassed in the vicinity of Grenada. The Iranians:

> I believe our government has a responsibility to go to the aid of its citizens, if their right to life and liberty is threatened. The nightmare of our hostages in Iran must never be repeated.
> (Address by President Ronald Reagan, October 27, 1983; *American Foreign Policy Current Documents 1983*, 1,411)

> Inaction [in Grenada] would have made more likely a hostage situation.
> (Address by Deputy Secretary of State Dam, November 14, 1983; *American Foreign Policy Current Documents 1983*, 1,268)

as well as the Soviets in alliance with the Cubans and other "terrorists":

> Grenada...was a Soviet–Cuban colony, being readied as a major military bastion to export terror and undermine democracy. We got their just in time.

> (Address by President Ronald Reagan, October 27, 1983; *American Foreign Policy Current Documents 1983*, 1,411)

These threats are global:

> The events in Lebanon and Grenada, though oceans apart, are closely related. Not only has Moscow assisted and encouraged the violence in both countries, but it provides direct support through a network of surrogates and terrorists. It is no coincidence that when the thugs tried to wrest control over Grenada, there were 30 Soviet advisors and hundreds of Cuban military and paramilitary forces on the island.
> (Address by President Ronald Reagan, October 27, 1983; *American Foreign Policy Current Documents 1983*, 1,411)

And global threats must be confronted, regardless of their location:

> Today, our national security can be threatened in far away places. It is up to all of us to be aware of the strategic importance of such places and to be able to identify them.
> (Address by President Ronald Reagan, October 27, 1983; *American Foreign Policy Current Documents 1983*, 1,411)

because failure to confront these threats proves to be harmful in the long-run:

> A ... lesson [of the Grenada military action]...of particular importance for the Sandinistas, is that in the absence of democratic institutions and legal safeguards, policy differences tend to degenerate into violence.
> (Address by Deputy Secretary of State Dam, November 4, 1983; *American Foreign Policy Current Documents 1983*, 1,424)

In addition to rallying the American public's support for the Grenadians by suggesting that the US citizenry and the Grenadians faced common enemies, the Reagan Administration's employment of anti-Soviet rhetoric inscribes the Grenadians as emerging democrats who are in need of protection from oppressive, anti-democratic forces. This move is particularly clear in the often commented-upon comparison of the US action in Grenada to the Soviet action in Afghanistan. Responding to the suggestion that these two incidents are analogous, President Reagan notes a number of differences. First, he argues that the Soviets had installed a government of their choice. Second, he argues that Soviet actions in Afghanistan were "against all the opposition of the Afghanistan people." And finally, he argues that while the Soviet action was an invasion, the US action was not.

> I know your frequent use of the word, invasion, this was a rescue mission ... And this was a rescue mission. It was a successful rescue mission, and the people have been rescued, and the Grenadians that

97

have been liberated, are down there delighted with and giving every evidence of appreciation and gratitude to our men down there.

(American Foreign Policy Current Documents 1983, 1,420)[5]

What the US rescued was the democratic future of the Grenadian people. One Reagan Administration official commented that as a result of the military action in Grenada, "Grenadians are now in a far better position to exercise their fundamental right to self-determination" (Address by Deputy Secretary of State Dam, November 14, 1983; *American Foreign Policy Current Documents 1983*, 1,268).

Ambassador to the United Nations Jeane Kirkpatrick elaborated on President Reagan's points in a speech some months later. Like the president, Kirkpatrick makes use of the liberator/oppressor dichotomy.

> the people of Grenada have welcomed US and OECS forces as liberators and are assuredly not fighting against them ... It was outside occupation forces – i.e., Cubans – who dug in and fought, leading to ongoing suffering.
>
> In Afghanistan, on the other hand, Soviet forces...are supported by a mere handful of communist party functionaries dependent on Soviet protection and are opposed by the general population, who form the resistance which has been fighting the Soviet occupation for 4 years.
>
> *(Current Policy 580:5)*

Should these subtle rejections by the Reagan Administration of any equation of the US military action in Grenada with intervention be lost, the administration supplemented these moves with a more legally based argument.

> Both the OAS Charter, in Articles 22 and 28, and the UN Charter, in Article 52, recognize the competence of regional security bodies in ensuring regional peace and stability. Article 22 of the OAS Charter in particular makes clear that action pursuant to a special security treaty in force *does not constitute intervention* or use of force otherwise prohibited by Articles 18 or 20 of the Charter. The OECS decided to act under the 1981 Treaty establishing the organization and creating a special security regime for the Eastern Caribbean.
>
> (My italics; Address by Deputy Secretary of State Dam, November 14, 1983; *American Foreign Policy Current Documents 1983*, 1,268)

After the invasion, the US-recognized legal representative of the Grenadian people announced:

> The people of Grenada...have welcomed the presence of troops [of the US/Caribbean security force] as a positive and decisive step forward in the restoration not only of peace and order but also of *full sovereignty.*
>
> (Brackets in original; my italics; Governor General Sir Paul Scoon of

98

> Grenada, quoted in a speech by Assistant Secretary for Inter-
> American Affairs Langhorne Motley, January 24, 1984; *Current Policy*
> no. 541:4)

The Governor General's message validates the US position that the military action was not a violation of the Grenadian people's sovereignty but rather of assistance to them in reaching their "full sovereignty."

The US invasion of Panama

The Wilsonian themes of self-determination and the realization of a people's sovereign identity are as central to the Bush Administration's discourse on the Panama invasion as they have been in US foreign policy discourse up to this point. What distinguishes their usage in the Panama invasion, however, is that the pursuit of the Wilsonian ideals shared by free peoples everywhere is not the goal of the Panamanian people alone. Rather, the Bush Administration discourse on the Panama invasion is as much about the preservation of Wilsonian ideals claimed by the US citizenry as it is about the realization of these ideals by the Panamanian citizenry. What makes this dual reading of self-determination possible is the discursive erasure of the domestic/ international boundary by the Bush Administration. The US invasion of Panama appears in US discourse as an act of domestic rather than foreign policy because who is represented as the community of judgment and foundation of sovereign authority in this discourse are located within US territorial boundaries.

The difficulty in determining whether the Panama invasion is a matter of US domestic or foreign policy can be traced to President Bush's justifications for military action. The primary justification for US military action was to protect Americans in Panama.

> Last Friday, Noriega declared his military dictatorship to be in a state of war with the United States and publicly threatened the lives of Americans in Panama. The very next day, forces under his command shot and killed an unarmed American serviceman; wounded another, arrested and brutally beat a third American serviceman; and then brutally interrogated his wife, threatening her with sexual abuse. That was enough.[6]
>
> General Noriega's reckless threats and attacks upon Americans in Panama created an imminent danger to the 35,000 American citizens in Panama. As President, I have no higher obligation than to safeguard the lives of American citizens. And that is why I directed our armed forces to protect the lives of American citizens in Panama and to bring General Noriega to justice in the United States.
>
> (*American Foreign Policy Current Documents 1989,* 720)

The president explained the US had four goals in Panama. In addition to safeguarding American lives, US goals in Panama were "to defend democracy in Panama, to combat drug trafficking, and to protect the integrity of the Panama Canal Treaty" (*American Foreign Policy Current Documents 1989*, 720). While safeguarding American lives and defending democracy are traditional justifications for US military actions abroad, as they appear in the Bush Administration discourse three goals outlined by President Bush – safeguarding American lives, defending democracy in Panama, and protecting the integrity of the Panama Canal Treaty – could be read as either a foreign or a domestic policy goal. The fourth policy goal – combatting drug trafficking – could be read as simultaneously a foreign and domestic policy goal. What identifies a policy goal as foreign or domestic is its point of reference in particular Bush Administration statements. What I suggest is that read independently, the first three goals appear to be foreign policy goals. Yet read from the standpoint of the fourth policy goal of combatting drug trafficking – and contextualized by the US "War on Drugs" – all US policy goals in Panama are domestic policy goals because the Bush Administration's point of reference is the US citizenry.

Panama Invasion as US foreign policy

As the President's statement outlining the US justifications for military action in Panama makes clear, "safeguarding American lives" in this context refers to insuring the safety of American citizens residing in Panama. This is a foreign policy goal because these US citizens are located outside of the territorial boundaries of the US.

The second US policy goal is to defend democracy in Panama. Defending democracy means recognizing the Endara government, thought to have won the May 7, 1989 elections, and removing obstacles to the democratic process in Panama. Both of these aspects of defending Panamanian democracy categorize it as a US foreign policy goal because defending democracy means defending the sovereignty of the Panamanian people. Therefore, the point of reference in the Bush Administration discourse is the Panamanian people. As one Bush Administration official explains, "The question before us has never been our commitment to Panamanian sovereignty nor is it today. For the sovereign will of the Panamanian people is what we are here defending" (Thomas R. Pickering, US Permanent Representative to the United Nations, December 20, 1989; *Current Policy* no. 1,240: 1).

The sovereign will of the Panamanian people is being defended against attempts to repress that will. Those making false claims to represent the sovereign will of the people – for example, dictators like General Noriega – appear in the Bush Administration discourse as obstacles to the democratic process in Panama. This distinction between the leader of a state and the people of a state, which can be traced back to the Wilson Administration, is reiterated by the Bush Administration.

> Today, we are once again living in historic times, a time when a great principle is spreading across the world like wild fire. That principle, as we all know, is the revolutionary idea that the people, not governments, are sovereign. This principle is the essence of the democratic form of government. It is by no means a new idea. But it is an idea which has, in this decade, and especially in this historic year – 1989 – acquired the force of historical necessity.
> (Luigi R. Einaudi, US Permanent Representative to the Organization of American States, December 22, 1989; *Current Policy* no. 1,240:2)

Authoritarian governments, whether in Eastern Europe or in Latin America, do not truly represent the sovereign will of the people. "General Noriega could not be permitted falsely to wrap himself in the flag of Panamanian sovereignty" (Pickering, December 20, 1989; *Current Policy* no. 1,240:2) because he did not truly represent the Panamanian people. Indeed, Noriega "suspended" the May 7 elections – never permitting the ballots to be counted – when it appeared that he would not be victorious. "The root cause of the crisis in Panama has been the struggle between Noriega and his thugs and the people of Panama. His ruthless cabal repeatedly obstructed the will of the Panamanian people which had been expressed in free elections" (Pickering, December 20, 1989; *Current Policy* no. 1,240:1).

From September 1, 1989, when the Endara government would have taken office until the invasion, the US refused to recognize any government in Panama. "The candidates chosen by the Panamanian people will not be allowed to take office today, as required by the Panamanian Constitution. Panama is therefore, as of this date, without any legitimate government" (President Bush, September 1, 1989; *Public Papers: George Bush 1989*, 1,131).

The US invasion put into place the legitimate government of Panama. As such, it liberated the Panamanian people and marked the rebirth of democracy (see *Public Papers: George Bush 1990*, 587–8). The administration's actions in Panama, like the actions of previous US administrations in Mexico, Russia, and Grenada, appear in this context to be clear expressions of US foreign policy.

The third US policy goal – defending the integrity of the Panama

Canal Treaty – also on the face of it appears to be a matter of US foreign policy. This is an international treaty negotiated between two sovereign nation states. It specifies that at least until the year 2000, the US shares operational and security responsibilities concerning the Canal with the Panamanians. Guaranteeing international access to the Canal was linked in the Bush Administration discourse to governmental stability in Panama. A Bush Administration official noted, "We must recognize ... that Panama's ability to responsibly pursue its own interests – and hence the long-term future of the canal – cannot be assured in the context of political instability." He went on to stress that democracy is "an essential element of political stability on the isthmus." Therefore, "Noriega's continuation in power is a threat ... And ... it will be the canal's users who ultimately must face the burden of bearing the costs" (Michael G. Kozak, November 2, 1989; *Current Policy* no. 1,126:2).

So long as Noriega governed Panama, he endangered the US "broad national interest" of maintaining "a safe, efficient, and neutral Panama Canal" (Kozak, November 2, 1989; *Current Policy* no. 1,126:2). The invasion occurred just eleven days before the administration of the canal was scheduled to be handed over to a Panamanian commission. This commission, because appointed by Noriega, could not legitimately represent the Panamanian people. Therefore, should the commission assume control of the Canal, the integrity of the Panama Canal Treaty would be in jeopardy.

Invasion of Panama as US domestic policy

The final US policy goal in Panama is to combat drug trafficking. In the Bush Administration discourse, combatting drug trafficking is not clearly a domestic or a foreign policy goal. While the Bush Administration holds, "This is a war as deadly and as dangerous as any fought with armies massed across borders (President George Bush, September 27, 1989; *Current Policy* no. 1,210:1–3, esp. 2)," the administration rhetoric on drugs erases any distinctions between what is domestic and what is international. According to the administration, drug trafficking "is a worldwide problem" that "threatens the security of nations" (Deputy Secretary of State Eagleburger, August 24, 1989; *Current Policy* no. 1,205:2). "The drug issue knows no national borders" (Deputy Assistant Secretary for International Organization Affairs John S. Wolf, October 17, 1989; *Current Policy* no. 1,219:1–2, esp. 2).

On drug issues, the administration refuses the domestic/international dichotomy, thereby making Noriega's drug–related indictments by two Florida grand juries less objectionable. Noriega is transformed from a head of state to a common domestic criminal. "The story these indictments tell is simple and chilling. It is the story of the same shameless excess in the criminal field that we have already seen in the political field" (Deputy Secretary of State Eagleburger, August 24, 1989; *Current Policy* no. 1,205:2). While Noriega's attorneys argued that as head of state, Noriega's activities – however objectionable to the US government – were protected by the doctrine of diplomatic immunity, "[t]he court ruled against them" (Eagleburger, August 24, 1989; *Current Policy* no. 1,205:3). The court here refers to a US court. The US justice system is the reference point which judges the status of a foreign head of state.

Bush Administration comments about the pursuit of Noriega during the short time when he eluded US military officials during the invasion underscore this. Addressing a question about the bounty on Noriega offered by the US government, President Bush responded:

> His picture will be in every post office in town. That's the way it works. He's a fugitive drug dealer, and we want to see him brought to justice. And if that helps, if there's some incentive for some Panamanian to turn him in, that's a million bucks that I would be very happy to sign the check for.
>
> (December 21, 1989; *Public Papers: George Bush 1989*, 1,731)

After Noriega "surrendered" to US officials, President Bush was asked if his administration's comments up to that point would prejudice Noriega's case. The President responded: "I would go back...to Watergate, where there were hearings held, charges made over and over again, editorials written and voiced; and yet the people received a fair trial. So, I am convinced that our system of justice is so fair that the person will get a fair trial" (*Public Papers: George Bush 1990*, 15). In this passage, the president equates the criminal allegations made against a foreign head of state with those made against US government officials. It is unimportant, according to the president, that the leader of one state undertook a military action against another state in order to capture the leader of the target state and "bring him to justice." The Bush Administration discourse views the allegations against Noriega as domestic matters. Bringing Noriega to justice means bringing Noriega to trial in the US. The community of judgment in this case will be a jury composed of US citizens. Justice here refers to US domestic justice not international justice.

This explains President Bush's reaction to Noriega's declaration of war against the US. Because of his refusal to take seriously Noriega's claim to be the sovereign authority in Panama, the President cannot take Noriega's declaration of war at face value. Asked at a news conference how he would respond to Noriega's declaration of war, President Bush answered, "Well, I don't respond to it ... It has not changed our view of him at all: he is an indicted narcotics dealer, and he ought to get out" (December 16, 1989; *Public Papers: George Bush 1989*, 1,711). The President's comments recast Noriega from his role as Panamanian head of state to a violator of US laws. This transforms the meaning of Noriega's declaration of war, as another Bush Administration official points out.

> There has been a good deal of mention about the fact that General Noriega declared war on the United States a few days ago. But the truth of the matter is that he declared war on my country a long time ago, from the moment he concluded his first deal with the narco-vermin who are wreaking havoc on our city streets and who seek to destroy our nation's most precious resource, its youth. Noriega and his ilk, whoever they are and wherever they may be, are guilty of nothing less than premeditated aggression against my country.
> (Einaudi, December 22, 1989; *Current Policy* no. 1,240:3)

As it is represented by the Bush Administration, Noriega's threat is not an international threat – a declaration of war by one sovereign state on another sovereign state – but a domestic threat – an illicit war against the very fabric of US society that long precedes his recent formal declaration. Acting in self-defense, the Reagan and Bush Administrations countered Noriega's narcotics trafficking with a war of their own – the "War on Drugs." Refusing to meet the challenges of the war on drugs would mean putting the future of democracy at risk:

> Freedom and democracy are in the ascendancy, yet they face formidable odds. Undoubtedly, drugs are among their mortal enemies, for freedom and democracy are universal ideals that speak to the dignity of every individual. And if these ideals are to be realized, every individual must make a contribution to his or her own society and to the world community. An individual caught in the grip of drugs becomes a slave – no longer a free or a responsible person. And the same thing can happen to entire nations.
> (Secretary of State James Baker, February 20, 1990; *Current Policy* no. 1,251:3)

Defending democracy – whether in Panama or in the US – is linked to combatting drug trafficking. This is why the "American people consider drugs the number one problem facing the United States" (Baker, February 20, 1990; *Current Policy* no. 1,251:3).

US discourse on the Panama invasion effectively subsumes Panamanian domestic affairs within the scope of US domestic policy.

Territorially, their domestic/international boundaries do not change; discursively, however, Panama is left with no domestic sphere distinct from that of the US. Thanks to this initial act of domestication, the invasion could be viewed as an internal act undertaken to consolidate one domestic space. The US invasion of Panama becomes an act of US domestic policy rather than foreign policy.

Two factors make the US domestication of Panamanian space possible. The first is historical. Panama's history as a sovereign nation-state cannot be separated from US history. It was the US desire for a canal in Central America in the early 1900s that lead the US to support a Panamanian claim of independence from Columbia. To this day, this act of genesis lingers in US–Panamanian relations. For it is the US that controls the vital circulatory systems of Panama – the Panamanian currency (US dollars) and the Panama Canal. Until the year 2000, the Panama Canal is US territory. It is not under the sovereign control of Panama. Mindful of these historical and geographical details, insuring the integrity of the Panama Canal Treaty can be viewed as a matter of US domestic policy.

Staged against a background of shared history is the second, more immediate factor. It is the US discursive claim to Panama couched in terms of the "War on Drugs." Panama's discursive domestication by the US drug war is highlighted when one attempts to identify the community of judgment in the invasion discourse. The Bush Administration discourse on the invasion always finds its point of reference in the US citizenry. Unlike the US military action in Grenada in 1983, the US did not direct its justification for intervention to some international community. No organization analogous to the Organization of Eastern Caribbean States was a conduit for a request for US military assistance. Nor did the US justify its military actions as a response to a request from Panamanian leaders who represented the sovereign will of the people. This was made clear in the Senate hearings on the Panama invasion. Asked by a Senator if the US military action in Panama resulted from an invitation, a Bush Administration official responded:

> Senator, the President made his decision based on his judgment that the security situation was deteriorating and a lot of Americans were at risk. Our charge met with the three candidates [Endara, Ford, and Calderon] and informed them of the President's decision. He did not ask them to invite us in and they did not invite us in. But they did indicate that they understood the President's decision and they welcomed it – with a heavy heart, but they welcomed it.
>
> But we do not claim that we took this action because they invited us in.
>
> (Bernard Aronson, Assistant Secretary of State for Inter-American

105

Affairs, December 22, 1989; Testimony before the Senate Armed Services Committee; *1989 Events in Panama*, 137–8)

A national, regional or international request for intervention was unnecessary because the US invasion of Panama was an internal matter. Only the US citizenry needed to be consulted and, in the event of military action, offered an explanation. "Operation Just Cause," the administration's code name for the invasion, was just by US domestic standards and was justified to the US public.

In the context of the "War on Drugs," all US goals in Panama are transformed from foreign to domestic policy matters. Safeguarding American lives refers to safeguarding Americans who reside in the US against drug trafficking. Defending the democracy of Panama means allowing the sovereign will of the Panamanian people to be expressed. This is linked to defending the Panamanian people from political instability brought about by an illegitimate head of state whose illegitimacy became clear to the US only once he faced indictments on drug trafficking in US courts. Finally, protecting the integrity of the Panama Canal Treaty is linked to defending US territory from threats of political instability. Overall, the US invasion of Panama is a matter of domestic policy because the community of judgment is the Bush Administration – a domestic community – and the foundation of sovereign authority is both the Panamanian people and the US people. As a domestic issue, then, the US invasion of Panama could not be viewed as intervention because a state cannot intervene in its own domestic affairs. Domestic "intervention" is not necessary because of a sovereign state's supposed monopoly on the use of legitimate violence. Furthermore, the invasion is not a violation of the sovereignty of the Panamanian people. Rather, it is the sovereign will of the people – Panamanian and American – that this internal action is undertaken to realize and preserve.

Foucauldian and Baudrillardian Analyses

In order to maintain a narrative which is consistent with US foreign policy since the Wilson Administration, Reagan–Bush administration discourses concerning Grenada and Panama produce representations of the people by first producing representations of international or regional communities. Regarding Grenada, the Organization of Eastern Caribbean States (OECS) is produced as the community of judgment. Yet rather than appearing as a legitimate cite of judgment, it is readily recognized as a convenient construction. Moving from Foucault's work on production to Baudrillard's work on seduction, I argue

106

that the open artificiality of the OECS community might be viewed as the manipulation of appearances (seduction) of a social or community in order to cover-up the nonexistence of any community and the failure of production. The same argument applies to "production" of the Grenadian people as the source of sovereign authority. The Grenadian people appear in US discourse as statistical abstractions which result from surveys or opinion polls. From a Baudrillardian perspective, the Grenadian people are not represented (because no meaningful representation of them can be produced) but simulated (because their images can be manipulated or seduced).

US discourse on the Panama invasion also operates according to a logic of simulation rather than representation. What makes the Panama invasion discourse so interesting is what the simulation of meanings does to the domestic/international boundary. In contrast to the Grenada discourse which reads as foreign policy because both US strategic concerns and a community of judgment lie outside the US, one cannot locate an international community of judgment in the Panama case. Judgments about foundational meanings are made by the Bush Administration. The foundational figure of sovereign authority, by this account, remains the people; however, because the Panama invasion is a matter of US domestic rather than foreign policy, the US people are the location of sovereign authority, and their simulation is vital in the Bush Administration discourse. The effect of reading the US invasion of Panama as a matter of domestic rather than foreign policy is to disrupt the narrative of intervention put in place by the Wilson Administration. In Foucauldian terms, the *trace* is insufficient to characterize US disciplinary acts in Panama, much less to investigate how discourses of sovereignty and intervention transform international relations theory.

Communities in the US discourse on Grenada

The international community invoked in the US discourse on the invasion of Grenada is the Organization of Eastern Caribbean States. As previously noted, OECS states were positioned in the invasion discourse as both indissolubly linked to Grenada concerning issues of self-determination due to regional associations as well as separate and distinct from Grenada so that they could objectively pass judgment on what did and did not constitute violations of sovereignty and intervention. Each position enabled the other and, combined, they established the OECS as the international community of judgment to which the US looked for legitimation of its actions in Grenada.

What enabled the OECS to perform as an external legitimating authority of US policy objectives were two things. One was the regional clout of the OECS. This clout rested on the size of the OECS – small and therefore presumably close-knit. Because Grenada was a member of this "family" of nations, it followed that the OECS might have more urgent concerns with events in Grenada than larger regional (Caricom or the OAS) or international (UN) organizations. Therefore, while the Caribbean region could have been inscribed in various ways along numerous dividing lines, the OECS as *the* Eastern Caribbean region was the most rhetorically if not militarily powerful.[7]

Because it was inscribed as *the* legitimate regional authority, the OECS appears in the invasion discourse as the logical center of decision-making about how to respond to the Grenada crisis. As the leading decision-making body, the OECS could and should determine what actions were legitimate (a military rescue mission of foreign nationals and, more importantly, of the self-determination of the Grenadian people) and which nation-states could legitimately aid in resolving the crisis (Barbados, Jamaica and the US). The OECS's rhetorical strength and military weakness made its request for US military assistance proper and necessary.

But if the legitimacy of the OECS as decision-maker is brought into question, so too are everything from US intervention justifications to foundational meanings like sovereignty and intervention. And if one reads around the invasion discourse, one finds that the legitimacy of the OECS's request for US military assistance in the region is a matter of open speculation.

It seems that the OECS's request was staged from the very beginning, when President Reagan and Prime Minister Charles, Chairperson of the OECS, shared top billing at the news conference in which the President announced that "on Sunday, October 23rd, the United States received an urgent, formal request from the ... Organization of Eastern Caribbean States to assist in a joint effort to restore order and democracy to ... Grenada" (October 25, 1983; *Public Papers: Ronald Reagan, 1983*, 1,505). Shifting our interpretive focus from events at center stage to events just off stage – from on stage to staging – what is suggested is that the OECS's part in the Grenada drama was at best co-authored with the US and was in production long before October 23, as well as long after that date. Furthermore, the staging of the OECS's request did more than put the OECS into public view. It constructed the OECS as *the* public or *the* social or *the* community of judgment in the invasion discourse.

The day after the invasion, remarks about the planning of the invasion suggested that the idea of an invasion may have been initiated by the Reagan Administration. US Ambassador to France Evan Galbraith commented "that the invasion was planned about twelve days before the events in Grenada" (quoted in Shahabuddeen, 1986:35). The ambassador's statement detracted from accusations circulating in the press that US involvement in Grenada was a diversionary tactic intended to shift public attention away from the loss of US marines to a terrorist attack in Lebanon. Yet this remark also implied that the US was planning a military action in Grenada long before the OECS offered an invitation for US assistance. As one scholar commented, the ambassador "later said he had 'misspoken.' But, whether he did or did not, was the statement attributed to him wrong?" (Shahabuddeen, 1986:35).

On the same day, in his address to the Barbadian people, Prime Minister Tom Adams elaborated on the decision-making process that led up to the invasion of Grenada. "On ... October 15, an official of the [Barbadian] Ministry of Defense and Security reported to me that he had been tentatively approached by a United States official about the prospect of rescuing Maurice Bishop from his captors and had been made an offer of transport" (October 28, 1983; *Documents on the Invasion of Grenada*, 1984: 35–6). The Prime Minister later retracted this statement.

A much later account of the events leading up to the invasion was offered by the Reagan Administration's Presidential Spokesperson, Larry Speakes.

> What we were claiming was that the OECS had invited us to participate in the invasion. The truth of the matter is that on Sunday, October 23, the day the "invitation" was issued, a representative of President Reagan, former US Ambassador to Costa Rica Frank McNeil, was on hand at the OECS meeting in Bridgetown, Barbados – just to make sure that when the invitation was issued, it was sent to the right address. You might also say that we RSVP'ed in advance ...
>
> Did we nudge the OECS nations into asking for US help? US forces were already in place before we were asked to participate. Before the request for help was received, the President, [Secretary of State] Shultz, and [National Security Advisor] Bud McFarlane were down in Augusta, working on plans in the late hours of Saturday and the early hours of Sunday morning, more than forty-eight hours before the invasion. So it's clear that we had set in motion and taken this opportunity to move against Grenada and clean it out before our allies could change their minds. (Speakes, 1988:161)

While these statements suggest that the US might have taken unilateral military action in Grenada, an OECS invitation for military assistance added to the legal justifications for a full-scale invasion. Journalist Ben Bradlee explained:

> Leaders of the [OECS] countries...were sent word by Washington that the chances of the United States intervening militarily in Grenada would be enhanced if the US received an official request from the OECS to do so. The leaders voted unanimously to make the request and, with Jamaica and Barbados, offered to provide a token three-hundred-man landing force to accompany an American invasion
>
> However transparent a justification, some felt the OECS' formal request for assistance and offer to participate in an invasion improved the administration's legal position with regard to international law while bettering its public relations position.   (Bradlee, 1988: 174–5)

Furthermore, the "invitation" to the US was drafted by Reagan Administration officials (see Shahabuddeen, 1986: 51).

Pre-scriptings were supplemented with post-scriptings. Only well after the invasion did the Reagan Administration append the OECS invitation with a Grenadian invitation:

> we were informed, on October 24, by Prime Minister Adams of Barbados that Grenada's Governor General, Sir Paul Scoon, had used a confidential channel to transmit an appeal to the OECS and other regional states to restore order on the island. The Governor General has since confirmed this appeal. We were unable to make this request public until the Governor General's safety had been assured, but it was an important element – legally as well as politically – in our respective decisions to help Grenada. The legal authorities of the Governor General were the sole remaining source of governmental legitimacy on the island in the wake of the tragic events I have described. We and the OECS countries accorded his appeal exceptional moral and legal weight. The invitation of lawful governmental authority constitutes a recognized basis under international law for foreign states to provide requested assistance.
> (Deputy Secretary of State Kenneth Dam, November 4, 1983; *Current Policy* No. 526: 2)

Prime Minister Adams made no mention of Scoon's invitation in his October 28th speech.

Both the Governor General's presumed request for assistance and his authority to make such a request have been questioned. The Reagan Administration spoke of the Governor General's legal authority as Queen Elizabeth's representative in Grenada (see statement by Assistant Secretary for Inter-American Affairs Langhorne Motley, January 24, 1984; *Current Policy*, no. 541: 3). Yet even if one accepts that the Governor General was the sole legal representative in Grenada from the time of Prime Minister Bishop's assassination,[8] other issues remain. Responding to a question about his relationship with the Revolutionary Military Council (RMC) which deposed the Bishop regime, Governor General Scoon replied:

> My relationship was always very good. They came to me soon after they assumed power and told me what their plans were. They kept me in the picture as to what they were doing. As to whether or not I approved of the things they wanted to do is a different matter. I do not wish to comment on that.
> (American Bar Association Committee on Grenada, "International Law and the United States in Grenada: A Report," Spring, 1984, *International Lawyer*, 18(2): 347)

The Governor General's remarks suggest not only that the RMC was in power in Grenada (in contrast to the anarchy assumption of US and OECS discourse) but also that he recognized the RMC authority. As one scholar noted, "No Commonwealth Governor–General has any *constitutional* authority to call in external armed intervention to remove a government which he recognises" (Shahabuddeen, 1986: 106).

Much more is at stake than the legality of the OECS or the Governor General to issue an invitation to the US for military assistance. Questions of legality quickly give way to questions of legitimacy. The potential illegitimacy of the OECS and of Governor General Scoon do more than put into question justifications for the US invasion of Grenada. They announce that the international community in the Grenada invasion is openly constructed. Its representation as a community first requires its production. Denials, such as those of the US ambassador to France and Prime Minister Adams of Barbados, confirm rather than refute suspicions that this international community – the OECS – is a fabrication, albeit a necessary one in the US discourse on the invasion. The OECS serves as one vital point of reference (the other being the Grenadian people) to which disputes about the meanings of sovereignty, intervention and statehood might be directed and ultimately settled.

Surrounding centrally staged officialized discourses pertaining to the invasion is open speculation that the OECS as an international site of judgment is a rhetorical *affect* rather than a community which existed as such outside of the invasion discourse. If the invasion discourse selects and stabilizes an international community – a reference point of judgments about meaning – then that community's selection and stabilization of meanings of sovereignty and intervention are not legitimate in and of themselves. The community's judgments mark the exercise not of truth but of power, employed in this

111

case to produce a truth. If the sovereignty/intervention boundary writes the state through specific interpretations of the meanings of sovereignty and intervention, then it would appear that power not truth determines where the boundaries of the sovereign state are to be drawn in this particular time and place. Power works through discourse to produce a community of judgment that interprets the truth within this discourse. By directing interpretive questions to the OECS, the US discourse establishes the OECS as the organization which can rightfully speak about and for the eastern Caribbean. Truth emanates from the OECS for no other reason than this is the role the OECS has been called upon to perform in the invasion discourse. This would be the conclusion of a Foucauldian analysis of the OECS as the community of judgment in the invasion discourse.

The open artificiality of the OECS as a community of judgment suggests more than that the OECS occupies the nexus of the power/ knowledge matrix as described by Foucault. Considered through the work of Jean Baudrillard rather than Michel Foucault, the Grenada discourse suggests that power no longer has a use value (a functional utility). Instead, power – to the extent that it continues to exist – retains only an exchange value because there is no truth, community of truth, or regime of truth to which power can refer. In other words, power fails to produce a meaningful truth. And what this failure signals is the breakdown of representation.

Reconsidered through Baudrillard's notions of simulation and seduction, the acts of legitimation in the US discourse on the Grenada invasion serve as reminders not so much of the illegitimacy of US actions but of the impossibility of legitimacy – of the emptiness of legitimacy. They remind us that meaning cannot be contained within rhetorical or military or state boundaries. Meaning is everywhere and nowhere. It is not that there is no meaning. It is that there is so much meaning that meaning is no longer "meaningful."

In this sense, the OECS as the international community in the invasion discourse functions less as an alibi for sovereignty than as what Baudrillard terms a "black hole" (1983b: 4) because rather than generating or deflect meaning, it absorbs all meaning. It is a reference point to which all parties in the invasion discourse refer but which does not produce any meaningful judgments. Openly artificial referents – domestic or international communities – announce that there is no obvious community or social which can ground interpretation. They announce that there is no stable foundation for any community because any transcendental signified can be substituted for another signifier. This is one way to account for the slippage in US discourse from the early announcement of the OECS invitation to a later announcement of the Governor General's invitation.[9]

Slippage also occurs with respect to the other vital referent in the invasion discourse – the Grenadian people. Initially described as true democrats repressed by authoritarian or totalitarian foes (e.g., the Soviets or Cubans), this description at times gives way to and at other times is supplemented by another representation of the Grenadian people as a statistical abstraction. Public opinion poll data litters the US discourse on the Grenada invasion. The Grenadian people's views about democracy, sovereignty, and the "rescue mission" were solicited and reported as percentages of opinion polls for and against specific statements.

> And the people of Grenada have spoken clearly of their happiness and relief at the restoration of legitimate, humane, democratic government.
> Grenadian views have just been reconfirmed by the first scientifically structured public opinion survey conducted in Grenada since the operation – a poll taken during the last week of December and the first week of January by St. Augustine Research Associates of Trinidad and Tobago. As reported in the January 20 edition of the Barbados newspaper, NATION, 86% of Grenadians queried agreed that the multinational operation was "a good thing." In the end, the big winners have been the people of Grenada.
> (Assistant Secretary for Inter-American Affairs Langhorne Motley, January 21, 1984; *Current Policy* no. 541:4)

Occasionally, the two dominant forms of representing the Grenadian people are combined. The following statement by President Reagan hints at the democratic nature of the Grenadian people by both opposing the Grenadian's reaction to US support to Soviet actions in Afghanistan and relying upon public opinion poll data to support his case.

> The Afghanistan people aren't meeting the soldiers with friendly waves and gifts of flowers and fruit over there. A CBS news poll shows that an overwhelming majority of the Grenadians – 91 percent – are glad the United States came to Grenada. I think that tells a lot about the differences between democracy and totalitarianism.
> (*Public Papers: Ronald Reagan, 1983*, 1,552)

A parallel move in found in comments by Ambassador to the United Nations Jeane Kirkpatrick.

> In Afghanistan ... Soviet forces ... are supported by a mere handful of communist party functionaries dependent on Soviet protection and are opposed by the general population ...

113

Not only did the students and the people of Grenada welcome the American, Jamaican, Barbadian, and OECS forces as liberators but a recent poll in Grenada – conducted by an American academic organization not famous for its support of the Administration – shows approximately 84% of the population both believe they were in danger and were glad that US troops came to Grenada.

(April 9, 1984; *Current Policy* 580:5)

This change in how the Grenadian people are "represented" is consistent with Baudrillard's account of simulation. If one had to locate the object of the Grenadian people in the invasion discourse, one would not "find" the Grenadian people. One would find instead opinions attributed to "them." As in the Wilson Administration's representations of the Mexican and Russian people in the discourse on the Mexican and Bolshevik revolutions, one might conclude that the Grenadian people are an imaginary referent – that their representation in the invasion discourse does not match up with their representation outside of that discourse. However, more is at stake here. Substituting "the Grenadian people" for "mass" in this passage by Baudrillard, I suggest:

> That the [Grenadian people are] an imaginary referent does not mean that they don't exist. It means that *their representation is no longer possible*. The [Grenadian people] are no longer a referent because they no longer belong to the order of representation. They don't express themselves, they are surveyed. They don't reflect upon themselves, they are tested. The referendum...has been substituted for the political referent. Now polls, tests, the referendum, media are devices which no longer belong to a dimension of representations, but to one of simulation. They no longer have a referent in view, but a model.
>
> (Baudrillard, 1983b:20)

Unlike the Wilson Administration discourse, the Reagan Administration discourse does not "represent" the people. It simulates the people. The Grenadian people are modeled after what the "real" Grenadian people – if they could be represented – might be expected to communicate. After the invasion, it is not meaningful to survey the Grenadian people – whose country is occupied by OECS and US troops – as to whether or not they approve of the invasion. The "opinions" of the "Grenadian people" serve once again to legitimate US policy after the fact. And what their simulation suggests is that legitimacy and illegitimacy are not meaningfully expressed in the invasion discourse. The domestic community of judgment about the legitimacy or illegitimacy of the invasion – the Grenadian people – cannot be represented as a community of judgment because the

114

Grenadian people never appear as a community or social in the invasion discourse. Put differently, the Grenadian people have no voice and render no judgments in the invasion discourse.

The Grenadian people, like the OECS, function in the invasion discourse as a "black hole" which attracts and refracts meaning but does not produce meaning. Even though US actions cannot be legitimated in the invasion discourse by a community of judgment (neither the OECS nor the Grenadian people), the invasion discourse is still directed toward these sites. But rather than act as foundations from which meaning and truth emanate, they instead serve as reminders that, in an order of simulation, discourses of truth are a dime a dozen. Amidst so much meaning, communities cannot anchor discourses of truth. They serve not as sites of judgment but sites of the implosion of meaning.

Panama

Since the Wilson era, US invasion discourse has contained all those elements recounted by President Wilson as central to justifying intervention – a commitment to self-determination, to the expression of sovereignty by free peoples, and to the opposition of authoritarian governments. US interventions are legitimated by the US claim to be acting on behalf of the foundation in a sovereign authority in the target state – the will of the people, sometimes expressed through democratically-elected governments. The US discourse on the Panama invasion draws upon many of the same discursive strategies. Yet US discourse in this case employs another discursive strategy – the domestication of Panama through the discourse on the War on Drugs.

The domestication of Panama and therefore the discursive erasure of a unique Panamanian sovereign space complicates traditional Wilsonian discourse in two ways. First, the domestication of Panama is at odds with US foreign policy discourse claiming to promote and preserve Panamanian sovereignty. Once Panama is discursively encircled, the American people and the Panamanian people share one sovereign space. It is no longer possible to distinguish Panamanian sovereignty from US sovereignty. But the Bush Administration would be going too far if it were to claim to *represent* the sovereign will of the Panamanian people. What the Bush Administration must do in order to avoid outright rejection of its discourse is to limit its discursive claim to Panamanian sovereignty to enabling the *simulation* of Panamanian sovereignty which can be distinguished from US sovereignty.

In typical Wilsonian style, the US military action in Panama was justified as defending the sovereignty of the people. According to the Bush Administration, the Panamanian people's sovereignty could not be freely expressed under a government headed by General Noriega because Noriega did not represent the will of the people. Noriega's removal from power was necessary to defend the Panamanian people whose will – in the Bush Administration discourse – is represented by the Endara government. This would seem to be consistent with Wilsonian discourse, for according to the Bush Administration the Endara government was democratically elected by the Panamanian people. But what you see is not always what you get in the Panama invasion discourse. Rather than *represent* the will of the Panamanian people, the Endara government *simulates* the will of the Panamanian people. The difference between representation and simulation here has important consequences for sovereignty and intervention.

In his statement announcing the military action in Panama, President Bush and his administration recognized the Endara government as the legitimate government of Panama. "The brave Panamanians elected by the people of Panama in the elections last May, President Guillermo Endara and Vice Presidents Calderon and Ford, have assumed the rightful leadership of their country" (December 20, 1989; *American Foreign Policy Current Documents 1989*, 720). Indeed, the Panamanian leaders were inaugurated the day of the invasion at the US compound. Since September 1, 1989 – when the Endara government was to have taken power under the Panamanian Constitution – the Bush Administration refused to recognize any government. Rather than recognize the Endara government, the Bush Administration declared that Panama was without any legitimate government (September 1, 1989; Statement on Panama-United States Relations; *Public Papers: George Bush 1989*, 1,131). Some statements by the Bush Administration suggest that recognition was withheld from the Endara government before the invasion because while it may have been the *de jure* government in Panama before the invasion, it was not the *de facto* government (see *Public Papers: George Bush 1989*, 1,412–13). Once US forces were able "to provide a stable environment for the freely elected Endara government" (President Bush, December 21, 1989; *Public Papers: George Bush 1989*, 1,729), questions surrounding the legitimacy of the Endara government were no longer an issue for the Bush Administration.

Yet the Endara government was not an elected government; it was a simulated government, as this exchange between a journalist and the President explains:

116

Q. Mr. President, you've referred to the elected government of Mr. Endara. As you know, there was never an accurate final count that confirmed that, even though most polls suggested he had probably won by a 3-to-1 margin. In talking with him, or in the future, have you encouraged him to seek again elections that would verify that he, indeed, or whoever, would be a legally elected President?

The President. I would encourage as much as their constitution calls for. But the election of Endara was, as you point out, so overwhelming, the vote count so high, that I don't think anybody can suggest somebody else might well have won that election.

Q. But, Mr. President, what I pointed out was that it was never final and it was never verified. It was stolen, as you point out.

The President. Well, because it was aborted by this dictator Noriega ... thwarting, frustrating the will of the Panamanian people. So, I think the international community that oversaw those elections, including a former President of the United States, felt that it went pretty well.

(December 21, 1989; *Public Papers: George Bush 1989*, 1,731)

About a month later, the subject was raised at another news conference.

Q. Back to Panama, sir. The election last May was the one that never really resulted in a full count because of General Noriega, yet that's the same election on which the Endara government is basing it legitimacy. Is it time, sir, for another election in Panama?

The President. Well, I think, fortunately, the Endara government has been endorsed by the Electoral Commission. They were kind of diverted from their normal course of business by Mr. Noriega a while back. But I think that's a matter for the Panamanians to decide. I think it would be a little bit outrageous for us to come charging in and tell them when they ought to have an election.

(January 25, 1990; *Public Papers: George Bush 1990*, 110)

The election results, although "stolen" by Noriega, were never really necessary to satisfy the Bush Administration. All that was required was that an electoral process, modeled on Western democracy, was undertaken. For such an electoral process demonstrates the people's desire to express their will. It demonstrates that the people want their will to be represented. Yet the entire electoral process which upholds political representation as its goal is a simulation.

The "representatives" of the Panamanian people – Endara, Ford, and Calderon – cannot trace their "victory" back to the Panamanian people because the Panamanian people do not appear as a community of judgment in the election discourse but as a mass. "Black box of every referential, of every uncaptured meaning, of impossible history, of *untraceable systems of representation*, the mass is what remains when the

117

social has been completely removed" (My italics; Baudrillard, 1983b:6–7). It is no longer a question of representing the real or the social but of simulating signs of the real. For while the social belongs to the order of representation because it produces meaning and has some sociological existence, the mass belongs to the order of simulation because it absorbs meaning and does not correspond to sociology:

> The mass is without attribute, predicate, quality, reference. This is its definition, or its radical lack of definition. It has no sociological "reality." It has nothing to do with any *real* population, body or specific social aggregate. Any attempt to qualify it only seeks to transfer it back to sociology and rescue it from this indistinctness which is not even that of equivalence (the unlimited sum of equivalent individuals: $1+1+1$ – such is the sociological definition), but that of the *neutral*, that is to say *neither one nor the other* (ne-uter).
> (Baudrillard, 1983b:5–6).

The appearance of victory for the Endara government was enough for the Bush Administration to pronounce this government legitimate. That the Endara government may well have won the election had the votes been counted is not the issue here. What is at issue is the manipulation of appearances, the following of the eye – what Baudrillard calls the *trompe l'oeil* (afterimage). In other words, the Panama election is not about the production of meaning but its seduction.

President Bush's remark that it would be "outrageous" for the US to tell the Panamanians to hold new elections contributes to the appearance that the Endara government was elected by due process. Yet exit polls, not ballots, are what "elected" the Endara government. The Endara government was put in power thanks to the efforts of the US because it *appeared* to have won the election. The Panamanian people did not express their will and elect representatives; they remained neutral (or, at the very least, their votes were neutralized). But their opinions on the election were surveyed, and these results are the basis upon which the Endara government claimed to represent the people.

Claims about the legitimacy or illegitimacy of the Endara government have no meaning because the community which was to have judged this issue – the Panamanian people – did not decide this question in the election. As was noted with respect to the Grenada invasion discourse, acts of legitimation do not settle questions of legitimacy; rather, they remind us that these questions cannot be settled because truth claims cannot be referred to and grounded by a community of judgment.[10]

But if the Endara government does not serve as the representative of the Panamanian people (as a second-order community of judgment),

118

then why does the Bush Administration's discourse treat it as if it did? Put differently, what is at stake in the Bush Administration's acceptance of the simulated Endara government? *Sovereignty*. The US claim to be acting on behalf of the sovereign will of the Panamanian people is contradicted by the US discursive domestication of Panama which cancels any Panamanian claim to sovereignty. For the US to both claim Panamanian sovereign space as well as seem to stop short of abrogating that space, it must simulate the will of the Panamanian people which it can defend.

The simulation of the Endara government is vital to the US invasion discourse not as a community which can produce judgments about US actions in Panama (recall that the Endara government did not "invite" the US to invade Panama) but as a simulacra, a "truth effect." The simulated Endara government makes it *appear* as if the Panamanian people have spoken and, in so doing, given their voice to elected representatives. In other words, the Endara government "effects" a Panamanian claim to sovereignty which has already been cancelled by the US discourse on the War on Drugs. In so doing, it provides the Bush Administration with the alibi so often used to justify interventions – defending the will of the people.

The second complication offered by the domestication of Panama has to do with the sovereignty/intervention boundary. Because US discourse on the War on Drugs transforms the Panama invasion into a domestic matter, no international community can judge where the sovereignty/intervention boundary lies and if it has been justly reinscribed. Combining foreign policy rhetoric with a discourse that nullifies domestic/international distinctions transforms the way in which the terms "sovereignty" and "intervention" function together.

Concerning invasion discourses considered up to this point, it has been argued that intervention justifications have redrawn the sovereignty/intervention boundary. In particular, it has been suggested that one key discursive move that marks this boundary is how and by whom the foundation of sovereign authority in the target state is represented. The US discourse on Panama could be interpreted following this argument by focusing on the inscription of the American people.

"Getting Noriega out" appears in Bush Administration discourse as defending the sovereignty not only of the Panamanian people but of the American people – here inscribed as a foundational figure of sovereign authority. Once again, the link here is made in the discourse on the War on Drugs. Ousting Noriega was one step taken by the Bush Administration to defend the American people from the interventionary policies of drug traffickers. President Bush asks, "[W]hat, in

119

God's name, would we ... call the international drug trade – and those who aid it and abet it – but intervention in our internal affairs?" (Bush, September 27, 1989; *Current Policy* no. 1,210: 2). This notion is expanded upon elsewhere.

> There are times when good principles force us to defend bad men. Some argue that this is the case with Noriega and Panama. They argue as if the principle of nonintervention requires us to accept whatever Noriega does.
>
> But nonintervention was never meant to protect individual criminals. It was never meant to promote intervention by drug traffickers in our societies against our families and children. It was never meant to prevent peaceful and diplomatic action by sovereign states in support of democracy. And it was never meant to leave the criminals free to savage the good and the good powerless to react.
> (Deputy Secretary of State Eagleburger, August 24, 1989; *Current Policy* no. 1,205: 6)

These passages could be viewed as a reversal of the sovereignty/ intervention dichotomy, requiring US troops to enter Panama to defend the sovereignty of the American people from the drug trafficking activities of General Noriega. Protecting American lives and sovereignty at home becomes a justification for military action abroad. And the representation of the people – Panamanian and American – plays a central role in the US invasion discourse.

Yet such an interpretation quickly encounters difficulties. For while US troops crossed the territorial boundary of Panama, the sovereignty/ intervention discursive boundary was not crossed – it was cancelled. US military actions in Panama did not so much violate Panamanian sovereignty as attest to Panamanian sovereignty having been subsumed within US domestic space. Nor were sovereign rights and responsibilities transferred from Panamanian domestic control (headed by an "illegitimate" leader) to the international control of an international community acting "on behalf of" the sovereign will of the Panamanian people. Panama was domesticated in the US discourse on the War on Drugs which cannot be disentangled from the US discourse on the Panama invasion. It is beside the point to ask questions such as "was Panamanian sovereignty violated?," "did the US military actions constitute intervention?," and "how was the sovereignty/intervention boundary redrawn?" These questions cannot be asked because they cannot be grounded. Put differently, in the Panama invasion discourse, there is no community of judgment to which to refer these questions. Within Panama, one finds only a simulated community of judgment (the Endara government); outside of Panama, no international community is invoked in the Bush Administration discourse.

In the Panama invasion discourse, "sovereignty" and "intervention" cease to function as dichotomous terms. It is no longer possible to oppose sovereignty and intervention because everyone seems to have a legitimate claim to sovereignty (the Panamanian people, General Noriega as *de facto* head of state, the Endara government, and the Bush Administration). Furthermore, everywhere there seem to be acts of intervention (US troops invade Panama and Panamanian drug traffickers transgress US boundaries). Following Baudrillard, if meaning is everywhere, it is also nowhere. Meaning implodes into mass, rendering meaning meaningless. Meaning can be endlessly exchanged, but it cannot be grounded.

It follows, then, that if sovereignty and intervention are everywhere, they are nowhere. If in the same discursive locale where one finds a "legitimate" claim to sovereignty, one also finds an equally "legitimate" example of intervention, sovereignty and intervention cannot be opposed to one another. Rather, they can be substituted for one another. Sovereignty is intervention, and intervention is sovereignty. In the Panama invasion discourse, their distinction and distinctness is erased with the domestic/international boundary. This boundary at least gave the impression that communities of judgment could be contained, identified, and dispatched to render judgments that would police the difference between these two terms. In the absence of anything but simulated communities, no one can authoritatively make such distinctions. Sovereignty and intervention are transformed from antonyms to synonyms. "Foreign" elections become matters of "domestic" policy. "Foreign" heads of state become common "domestic" criminals.

Sovereignty and intervention have exceeded their saturation points. They no longer produce meaning. Instead, sovereignty is transformed from a meaningful referent represented by various signified (monarchical authority or the will of the people, for example) into mass where meaning is absorbed. Intervention is attracted to this mass. But because intervention can no longer be opposed to sovereignty, it cannot guarantee meaning. Intervention too is absorbed into sovereignty's mass.

It is no longer possible to represent the sovereignty/intervention boundary and "write" the state via representational practices. "Sovereigntyintervention" (now one term) respect no boundary. What remains of "sovereigntyintervention" when one moves from representation to simulation? Again following Baudrillard, I suggest that in an order of simulation, what is at stake is not the representation of sovereignty (for this is no longer possible) but access to and simulation of sovereignty. What remains are the signs of sovereignty and a simulated sovereignty/intervention boundary.

7 SYMBOLIC EXCHANGE AND THE STATE

> Only signs without referents, empty, senseless, absurd and elliptical
> signs, absorb us   Jean Baudrillard[1]

The state is a sign without a referent. Most international relations theorists argue otherwise. They suggest that the state has a referent, and this referent is "sovereignty." But, as this study suggests, sovereignty also requires a referent. Various referents have been proposed throughout history, the most powerful of which have been god and the people. Whether regulated by the law of nature or the law of equivalence, an exchange of sovereign authority presumably takes place between god and a monarch or the people within a state and their political representatives. In these ways, states acting in international affairs may "refer" to one or another sovereign foundation as the source of their sovereignty and legitimacy.

As argued in the Foucauldian analyses of interventions by the Concert of Europe, Wilson Administration, and Reagan-Bush Administrations, to guarantee terms of reference one must first produce them. Sovereign foundations are produced as signifieds in order to make representational projects possible, in order to allow sovereignty and the state to refer to some original source of truth. This is a fundamental way in which power and knowledge function in a logic of representation.

From a Foucauldian perspective, the story these interventions tell is one of how disciplinary power is involved in the production of sovereign foundations. Foucault's three modalities of punishment – the mark, the sign, and the trace – correspond to the intervention practices undertaken by the Concert of Europe, the Wilson Administration and the Reagan-Bush Administrations respectively. Each intervening power was constituted as one community of judgment about the true meanings of sovereignty and intervention and the true location of sovereign authority. As disciplinary communities, each acted on behalf of the true sovereign – the Concert acting in the name of the monarch, the Wilson and Reagan–Bush Administrations acting in the name of the people – to *mark* the bodies of deviant Spain and Naples, proliferate the *sign* of sovereignty in Mexico and Siberia, and *trace* democratic ideals held by the Grenadian and Panamanian people back to Wilsonian traditions so they could be revived and reinforced.

These cases illustrate Foucault's general point that "sovereignty and disciplinary mechanisms are two absolutely integral constituents of the general mechanism of power in our [modern] society" (1980a:108). Within a logic of representation, discourses of truth (sovereignty) legitimate uses of power (disciplinary acts of intervention). However dispersed, power refers to truth. While the signifier/signified relationship within the sign can be displaced (state refers to sovereignty which refers to the people), displacements must come to rest at some transcendental signified (a sovereign foundation or source of sovereign authority). The basic relationship within the sign (signifier/signified) is unchanged by these displacements. As for intervention and sovereignty, they are paired as signifier/signified. Intervention (disciplinary power) refers to sovereignty or truth (foundational figures of sovereign authority).

By focusing on the production of meanings in different historical periods, a Foucauldian approach takes up an aspect of sovereignty that is neglected by most international relations theorists – how changes in the foundations of sovereign authority affect the state. Sovereignty has various meanings depending upon how it is grounded. When foundational figures of sovereign authority change, so too do the meanings of sovereignty. In most international relations theory, "sovereignty" performs as a referent for the term "state" so long as "sovereignty" stabilizes the meaning of "state." The theoretically important work of considering how variations in the meaning of sovereignty affect the state is necessarily overlooked because such investigations promise to destabilize the state.

Intervention as disciplinary power participates in the production of a sovereign foundation so that a state may function in international society as a sign of the political representation of its population. What a state must do in order to be sovereign is to organize its affairs in such a way that its foundation of sovereign authority is authorized to speak for its particular domestic community in international affairs. Internationally, a state must look to an external community of sovereign states to authorize its claim to sovereignty. What a Foucauldian approach to state sovereignty underscores is that within a logic of representation, being a state depends not only upon political representation but also upon symbolic representation. The foundations of sovereign authority and the communities which judge them to be legitimate must be produced (symbolically represented) before they can be politically represented.

Paradoxically, while acts of intervention often destabilize international politics, intervention discourses participate in the production and re-stabilization of concepts like the state and sovereignty. Intervening states offer justifications for their actions to a supposed international community and couch their justifications in terms of acting on behalf of the sovereign authority in the target state. This has three effects. It produces an international community of judgment. It produces a sovereign authority in the target state. Finally and most importantly, it participates in drawing the sovereignty/intervention boundary. Determining what is legitimately within the domain of a state's sovereign authority and what lies beyond it produces a particular historically and temporally situated state with specific competencies. Drawing the sovereignty/intervention boundary, then, produces, represents or writes the state.

What happens to the state when a logic of representation breaks down and we move to a logic of simulation? Jean Baudrillard's work suggests that there are fundamental differences between a logic of representation and a logic of simulation. Among the most important differences concerns the relationship between truth and power. In a logic of simulation, power is not opposed to truth (as much international relations theory holds) nor is it productive of truth (as Foucault suggests). Applied to sovereignty, both of these descriptions of truth and power require that a foundational figure and source of sovereign authority (truth) is either repressed or produced by power. In a logic of simulation, by contrast, power neither represses nor produces truth. Instead, truth is seduced. Its appearance is manipulated. In Baudrillard's terms, truth appears as a simulacrum (a truth effect) but not as a referent or signified. This is what the interventions by the Reagan–Bush Administrations in Grenada and Panama exemplified. Whether simulated regional communities (the Organization of Eastern Caribbean States), simulated domestic communities (the Grenadian and American peoples), or simulated governments (the Endara government of Panama), each is a simulacrum, a truth effect. "Pure appearances, they have the irony of too much reality" (Baudrillard, 1990:61). In these cases, "foundations" which appear to be "too real" (or openly artificial) serve to bring truth, its production, and its representation into question.

In an order of simulation, the distinction between what is real and

125

what is artificial cannot be produced because too much reality is the same as no reality. The terms "real" and "unreal" collapse into one term due to the abundance of "reality." No boundary exists between them. "Realunreal" and "truthpower" each circulate as one term. They can no longer be represented because "the distance between the real and its double, and the distortion between the Same and the Other, is abolished" (Baudrillard, 1990:67). Their appearances can be manipulated (seduced). For example, exit polls can simulate elections in Panama, and opinion polls can simulate the Grenadian people. But neither "real" and "unreal" nor "truth" and "power" can function as opposed terms. Instead, they circulate as openly artificial signs and as simulacrum (truth-effects).

Simulation changes the structure within the sign. Rather than having a signifier/signified relationship within a sign (as exists in a logic of representation), signs in a logic of simulation are composed of a chain of signifiers. Terms are not opposed to one another because opposition is not possible without boundaries. Rather, signifiers are interchangeable and reversible. They can appear on either side of the signifier/signified "dichotomy." These re-structured signs result from both the inability to police distinctions between terms and the inability to ground "truth" in some transcendental signified or foundational figure. Without referents, signs are transformed from "meaningful" as they are in a logic of representation to "empty, senseless, and elliptical." Writes Baudrillard, "Seduction lies with the annulment of the signs, of their meaning, with their pure appearance" (1990:76). Signs continue to circulate, and their exchange continues; however, rather than exchanging for "the real," signs now exchange for signs of the real – for truth-effects (the Endara government), models (the Grenadian people as opinion polls), and other openly-artificial simulations of the real (the Organization of Eastern Caribbean States as the legitimate regional community of judgment in for the Grenada invasion).

Theorizing the relationship between "state sovereignty" and "intervention" in a logic of simulation requires that we cease to assume representational relationships (sign = signifier/signified) and pose representation as a question. Instead of asking "what is represented?" we now ask "how does the representation assumption affect our understandings of state sovereignty and intervention?"

In a logic of simulation, sovereignty does not function as a meaningful referent for the state which can be traced to various transcendental signifieds (god or the people). Sovereignty has no "natural" or "use" value in simulation. What sovereignty does retain is sign value. Sovereignty's place within the sign is as a signifier in a chain of signifiers, not

126

as a foundational term. The same holds for its opposite in a logic of representation – intervention. In simulation, sovereignty and intervention cease to function as opposed terms – as signifier/signified. They become two signifiers which can be substituted for one another. In other words, the difference between them is erased. They collapse into one term, "sovereigntyintervention."

The Bush Administration's intervention into Panama is the clearest example of this collapse. Protecting the sovereignty of the Panamanian people meant invading the sovereign state of Panama in order to capture its Head of State General Manuel Noriega and bring him to the United States where he would stand trial for violating US laws. Although there were indications of the pending collapse earlier (in the Concert invasions and particularly during the Wilson Administration), the US invasion of Panama nullifies any difference between sovereignty and intervention. In so doing, it is fatal to the system of representation which requires some value (sovereignty) to insure the value of terms within the system. Baudrillard writes, "The process of value is irreversible. Only reversibility then, and not release or drift, is fatal to the system. And this is exactly what is meant by the term symbolic 'exchange'" (Baudrillard, 1988: 124).

In such a system of symbolic exchange, sovereignty is no longer something to be represented but something to be accessed through simulation. Sovereignty becomes a code. It is a bundle of practices which, when performed, grant specific rights and responsibilities to a nation-state. It is not important that a "sovereign" nation-state cannot meet the "tangible" requirements of sovereignty – ultimate authority over a territory occupied by a relatively fixed population and independence internationally. What become important are the signs of sovereignty – the ability to access the code of sovereignty (obtain diplomatic recognition as a "sovereign" state or membership in the United Nations)[2] and the ability to simulate the foundation of sovereign authority (the people).

Accordingly, states continue (in part) to be written effects of the sovereignty/intervention boundary. However, what it means to "write" the state is different in a logic of simulation than it is in a logic of representation. In a logic of representation, a boundary "truly" exists between sovereignty and intervention, and this boundary insures the distinction between these two terms. It allows them to perform as opposites. Because sovereignty defines the domain of a state's legitimate authority and intervention marks the outer limit of this authority, the sovereignty/intervention boundary is the location of the state. In a logic of simulation, because sovereignty and intervention are interchangeable terms which respect no boundary, a boundary between them must be simulated in order to simulate the state. Simulation of the sovereignty/intervention boundary is performed with recourse to what Baudrillard calls the abili function.

Baudrillard argues that one way to assert the "realness" (and distinctness) of something like sovereignty is by contrasting it with its "hyperreal" (too real to be its opposite) counterpart, intervention. Within a system of symbolic exchange in which "reality" operates according to principles of "hyperreality" and simulation – where signifiers exchange for other signifiers and where questions of "real" and "imitation" lose their meaning – recognizable imitations are circulated in order to give the appearance that some "real" signified exists. His illustrations are Disneyland (which is presented as fantasy in order to suggest that the rest of America is "real") and Watergate (an example of scandal and transgression against the law circulated as evidence that America is grounded by laws). One effect of practices which attempt to rescue the "reality principle" and ground a logic of representation is that these practices put into circulation signs which endlessly refer back to themselves or other signs and – if recognizably "unreal" – suggest that a "real" exists. Additionally, these practices deflect attention away from the self-referentiality of simulation in which signifiers are interchangeable.

As the Grenada and Panama interventions illustrate, no "domestic community" or ground can be distinguished from other communities and made to serve as the foundation of sovereign authority within a state. Yet sovereignty is relied upon by diplomats and theorists to ground understandings of international practice. Diplomats forever call upon sovereignty in reference to their particular international practices, but the sovereignty to which they refer refers only to itself. That sovereignty appears to refer back to a "domestic community" suggests that a "domestic community" exists. In this sense, sovereignty is an alibi for a "domestic community."

Yet sovereignty also needs an alibi. Otherwise, it will be recognized that sovereignty refers only to itself. According to diplomats and international relations theorists, to be sovereign a state must be recognized as sovereign by other sovereign states. But mutual recognition – self-reference – is not enough to rescue the "reality principle." More than access to the code of sovereignty is required. Diplomats and theorists turn to intervention. For intervention to be meaningful, sovereignty must exist because intervention implies a violation of sovereignty. To speak of intervention, then, is to suggest that sovereignty does exist. In Baudrillard's terms, intervention or transgression proves sovereignty or the law.

The circulation of hyperreal signifiers as alibis for sovereignty and intervention simulates the sovereignty/intervention boundary. Writing the state in an order of simulation requires simulating the sovereignty/intervention boundary and other boundaries (e.g., domestic/international, inside/outside, citizen/foreigner). International relations theories which take these boundaries as givens and continue to theorize state sovereignty within a logic of representation fail to explain how the modern (or postmodern) state is written. Simulation radically problematizes boundaries, foundations, and representational modes of exchange. It is only through discursive practices – in this case the circulation and symbolic exchange of sovereignty and intervention as hyperreal signs – that the "distinctness" and "opposition" of these terms is made possible, and the state is written. In an order of simulation, what a state must do in order to be sovereign is control the simulation of its "source" of sovereign authority and simulate a boundary (e.g., sovereignty/intervention, domestic/international) which marks the range of its legitimate powers and competencies. Investigating state sovereignty, then, requires investigating how states are simulated.

NOTES

1 Writing the state

1 Grieco (1988) and Kegley (1993) illustrate these points for neorealism and neoidealism.
2 Recent investigations of the sovereign state include Caporaso (1989), Carnoy, (1984), Evans et al. (1985), Hall and Ikenberry (1989), Held (1989), Jackson (1990), James (1986), Onuf (1991), and Walker (1993).
3 For a discussion of essentially contested concepts, see Connolly (1987).
4 See, for example, Robert Jackson's analysis of sub-Saharan African states as quasi-states (1990). Also see Naeem Inayatullah's critic of Jackson's work in an effort to combine theories of state sovereignty and political economy (1993).
5 Although I at times refine what I mean by "space" by using the term "territory," I do not mean to suggest that these two terms are synonyms. Geographers define "space" as distance and "territory" as a specific spatial relationship (see Johnston, 1986). Robert Sack defined "territoriality" as "the attempt by an individual or group (x) to influence, affect, or control objects, people and relationships (y) by delimiting and asserting control over a geographic area" (Sack, 1983:56). Writing elsewhere, Sack argued, "Territoriality is easy to communicate because it requires only one kind of marker or sign – the boundary" (Sack, 1981:64). Relying upon these definitions, some geographers then go on to view the state as "necessarily a set of territorial strategies" and question why this is so (Johnston, 1986:565). For an illustration of how these concerns have been explored in international relations theory and how notions of space and territory are being transformed, see Connolly (1993), Luke (1989 and 1991), and Ruggie (1993).
6 For an analysis of state institutionalizations of a monopoly on the legitimate use of violence, see Thomson (1994).
7 This might be argued with reference to the work of Robert Keohane and Robert Gilpin, for example, which traces the realist tradition in international relations back to Thucydides. For accounts of the emergence of sovereignty as but one type of authority and for competing historical forms of authority, see Wight (1977), Poggie (1978), and Hinsley (1986).
8 I use the term "supposed international community" to convey the notion that no unambiguous international community exists. Indeed, the very practice of justifying intervention practices to a community participates in the constitution of that community. Unlike much of the regime and/or

norms literature, this analysis does not politicize foundational figures only later to take some international community as its unambiguous point of reference. For instances of how the regime/norm literature takes communities as already given, see Keohane (1984), Ruggie (1989), and Thomson (1990).

9 This intellectual problem – how do changes in collective understandings of sovereignty transform (theoretical understandings of) states – is not unlike that of Kathryn Sikkink. While our work differs in theoretical approach and topic, I agree with Sikkink that "If sovereignty is a shared set of understandings and expectations about the authority of the state and is reinforced by practices, then a change in sovereignty will come about by transforming understandings and practices" (Sikkink, 1993:414).

10 Deborah Welch Larson's work is a notable exception to this line of thinking. See Larson (1985).

11 By interpretive communities, I am referring to what Foucault called a "site of judgment." For a discussion of this, see Foucault (1979) and Dreyfus and Rabinow (1982).

12 In *Writing Security* (1992), David Campbell analyzes another aspect of how identities are "written" in foreign policy. He argues that states are constituted as sovereign identities in part through their identification of enemies. Also see Richard Ashley (1989a).

13 Herz later retracted this argument. See Herz (1969).

14 Although most of these scholars (with the exception of Walker) posit the state as ontologically prior to their discussions about the state's dwindling hold on sovereign authority, their arguments undercut this primary assumption. For an analysis of how this is so, see Ashley (1989b).

15 Political representation should not be confused with notions of democracy. While this is one form that political representation might take, it is not the only or necessary form.

16 For a discussion of this problem as it applies to state sovereignty, see Ashley (1989b).

17 This does not mean that monarchs ceased to exist. Contemporary global political life illustrates that they have not. However, contemporary monarchs rarely are held to be the source of sovereign authority nor the representations of god on earth. What power they do hold they generally share with their citizenries.

18 Derrida speaks of putting words under erasure. For a discussion of Derrida's notion, see Spivak (1976) and Culler (1982).

19 Wendt later modified his position. See Wendt (1992).

20 Markus Fischer (1992) argues that there exists historical continuity between the Medieval and Modern international systems because there is no disjuncture between communal discourse (which should lead to cooperation) and conflictual practices undertaken by states in these systems. Contrary to Fischer's assertions, this does not nullify the efforts of critical theorists. Fischer asserts that the neorealist vs. critical theorist debate has neorealists on the side of continuity and critical theorists on the side of change. What Fischer failed to take into account is the variety of positions held by those he labels "critical theorists" (including John Ruggie, Robert Cox, and

Richard Ashley). In particular, Fischer overlooks the fact that poststructural theorists reject the continuity/change dichotomy. For these theorists, the issue is not "does change dominate continuity?" Rather, these theorists attempt to think about international relations theory beyond the narrow constraints of the continuity/change dichotomy.

21 This is not to suggest that international law scholars have not contributed greatly to sovereignty debates. They have done so, however, by asking questions different from those addressed in this study. For a brief outline of international law themes and their relationship to conventional international relations studies of state sovereignty, see Walker (1993:173–4).

2 Examining the sovereignty/intervention boundary

1 Thinking about state sovereignty in this way does not lead to equating the terms statehood and sovereignty. For example, during instances of intervention, sovereignty may or may not be invested in the target state. What is in question during such times is sovereignty and not statehood. States continue to exist under these conditions even when their sovereignty is in question.

2 Little suggested the sovereignty/intervention boundary as a beginning point for analysis. See Little, 1987.

3 I borrow this phrase from Edmund S. Morgan's book, *Inventing the People: The Rise of Popular Sovereignty in England and America*. See Morgan, 1988.

4 I do not mean to imply that until the US invasion of Grenada, interpretive communities were not constructed. Rather, because the US justified its activities to such an unlikely community, the constructedness of the OECS as an interpretive community was an open secret.

5 Geertz acknowledges that he is borrowing these terms from Gilbert Ryle's writings (1949).

6 I discuss the notion of a supposed international community as an interpretive sight of judgment in traditional studies of intervention below.

7 Little's complaint is that that which constitutes a challenge to state sovereignty – intervention – is too narrowly defined in international relations theory. It must be broadened to include economic as well as military intervention, for example (Little, 1987:54).

8 Little's blindness to this point is due to his own work on intervention from a traditional perspective. In his book, *Intervention: External involvement in civil wars* (1975), Little breaks with the traditionalists who view intervention as a form of deviance and instead regards intervention "as a result of autistic thinking: a systematic distortion of reality" (1975:xii). Even so, underlying this autism is the norm of nonintervention which is attributable to both an international society (1975:18) and a stable notion of sovereignty.

9 That traditional analyses of intervention do not escape a logic of representation is not surprising when one reconsiders Geertz' explanation of culture as a semiotic concept. For Geertz, a logic of representation still applies. What Geertz adds is an awareness that different symbolic orders function simultaneously in different historical and geographical locales.

132

For behavior to be meaningful, one must access those symbolic orders which convey meaning. For Geertz, signifiers do represent signifieds within a symbolic order. To this extent, Geertz' arguments adhere to a logic of representation.

3 Interpretive approaches

1 Foucault elaborates what he does and does not mean by power in his *History of Sexuality, Volume 1*. Power for Foucault is a "multiplicity of force relations" and "that name that one attributes to a complex strategical situation in a particular society" (1980b: 92, 93). However vague Foucault is in describing what power is, he compensates for by his insistence about what power is not. Power is not an institution, or a structure, nor a possession such as strength. Power is not exterior to other types of relations (economic, knowledge, sexuality) but productive of those relations. It is not generated from above but is everywhere and therefore permeates the matrix of relations. Finally, power is both intentional and nonsubjective (1980b: 92–6). Elsewhere, Foucault expresses this last aspect of power when he says, "People know what they do; they frequently know why they do what they do; but what they don't know is what what they do does" (quoted in Dreyfus and Rabinow, 1983: 187).
2 In *Discipline and Punish* (1979) and *The History of Sexuality, Volume 1* (1980b), Foucault does describe symbolic orders that might well be characterized as postrepresentational. As readers familiar with the writings of Foucault and Baudrillard will no doubt observe, my distinction between Foucault and Baudrillard's third orders as representational and postrepresentational is an overstatement of the differences in their work. As opposed to Baudrillard's third order, Foucault's order could be more accurately described as normalizing/disciplinary/performative. However one describes it, Foucault's third order is not an order of simulation. It is this last point that my terminology attempts to underscore.
3 Baudrillard's orders of simulation arose from his engagement with Marxism, particularly from his efforts to theorize exchange value from the position of objects. For general discussions of Baudrillard's work, see Mark Gain (1991a and 1991b).
4 Baudrillard describes a fourth order of simulation as well. See Baudrillard (1992).
5 Baudrillard defines a simulacrum as "a truth effect that hides the truth's non-existence" (1990: 35).
6 Elsewhere, Baudrillard expresses these ideas a bit differently. He writes, "seduction represents mastery over the symbolic universe, while power represents only mastery of the real universe" (italics in original; Baudrillard, 1990: 8).
7 I could have read these first two cases through Baudrillard's first two order of simulation as well. While I do occasionally employ Baudrillard's language to explain these cases, I focus on the Foucauldian question "how is representation possible?" in order to accentuate the break between Foucault and Baudrillard regarding representation and simulation.

4 Concert of Europe interventions

1 France was later included in the Alliance, as were many other states. See Albrecht-Carrie (1968:34).
2 While debate on these questions continued past 1823, the Concert did not continue to exist past 1823.
3 For thorough considerations of the norm of nonintervention, see Vincent (1974) and Little (1975).
4 Castlereagh's position underscores that while there was considerable agreement among Concert powers about "the legitimacy and appropriateness of class rule" (Albrecht-Carrie, 1968:6), the degrees of difference with which "class rule" was put into practice were core concerns among powers and should not be minimized.
5 See in particular Schroeder (1962) and Kissinger (1964).
6 Webster (1958) paints an equally glowing picture of Castlereagh.
7 For example, the kings of both Spain and Naples agreed to share power with the people as the result of revolutionary events in their respective states, and both swore allegiance to the Spanish Constitution of 1812 – a constitution which would replace absolute monarchy with popular sovereignty.

5 Wilson Administration actions

1 Jennings, 1965:56.
2 This corollary was invoked by Theodore Roosevelt in December of 1904 in defense of United States intervention in the Dominican Republic.
3 The abbreviation *FRUS* stands for *Foreign Relations of the United States*. I use this abbreviation throughout.
4 Numerous draft agreements where exchanged and modified between late March and mid-April of 1916. At issue were, for example, United States troop use of Mexican railroads, a ban on United States troops in Mexican towns, and the radius of United States troop movements in Mexican territory. Negotiations were suspended by the Mexican government on April 12, 1916.
5 This cable is dated June 21, 1916.
6 President Wilson responded to Secretary Lansing's first cable saying, "I agree to all of this. I was myself about to say something to you to the same effect" (FRUS, 1916:559).
7 Throughout this discussion of events in Russia and the newly formed Union of Soviet Socialist Republics, I will use the European calendar for dating events rather than the Russian calendar.
8 In fact, the United States government was the first to grant formal recognition to the Provisional Government. It did so on March 22, 1917. See FRUS (1917:1,208 and 1,211).
9 This kind of logic is evidenced in many US cables. See FRUS (1917 and 1918).
10 Characteristically, Secretary of State Lansing made harsher use of the French Revolution analogy in reference to the Bolshevik Revolution. See Baker and Dodd (1925–1927, vol. 5:49–50).

134

11 Early in the Bolshevik Revolution, Wilson shared this view with Colonel House. Later, however, he was persuaded by the harsher anti-Bolshevik position taken by Secretary of State Lansing. For a discussion of this transition in Wilson's thinking, see Levin (1968: chapter 2).

12 For a discussion of the irreconcilable differences between Wilsonianism and Leninism, see Levin (1968: chapter 1).

13 This is Lansing's assertion.

14 The German army never did advance far enough to threaten the railway; however, at the time, the Allies feared that because the German army would meet little resistance from the Russians on the old Eastern Front, the German army potentially could secure the railway.

15 My usage of this term follows its usage by N. Gordon Levin, Jr. Levin used the terms liberal-internationalism and liberal-capitalist internationalism interchangeably

> to refer to the Wilsonian vision of a global situation beyond power politics to be characterized by open world trade and by great power co-operation within a framework of world law and inter-national-capitalist commercial relations. In Wilson's view, moreover, the projected triumph of such a liberal-capitalist world order over traditional imperialism would represent the realization of America's liberal mission to lead mankind to a victory over the unenlightened past. (Levin, 1968: 3).

16 While this distinction between "political" and "military" is arbitrary, most importantly because any military action is also political, I use these terms because they are the terms used in the US cables.

17 United States Consul Poole at Moscow cabled the Secretary of State in mid-June of an invitation to intervention by an unnamed member of the Siberian Cooperative Societies. Poole reports:

> A confidential invitation to the Allies to intervene has, however, heretofore been considered a matter for the future. Now that the Siberian government, which has the hearty support of the Cooperatives, must be prepared to fight not only upon the Soviets but Germany, which is directing German war prisoners against the Czecho-Slovaks, he [unnamed] does not hesitate, although without states authority to do so, to invite on behalf of the Siberian Union of Cooperatives immediate Allied intervention in Siberia ... (FRUS, 1918–1918, Russia, vol. 2: 210–11).

It is unclear from United States cables whether or not this invitation was taken seriously. I found no discussion of this invitation in the cables.

18 See "Statement of Recommendations Concerning the Russian Situation," authored by Raymond Robins, for details on American economic cooper-ation with Russia as part of a broader political program (FRUS, 1914–1920, Lansing Papers, 1931–1937, vol. 2: 366–72).

19 Sir William Tyrrell made this remark to Sir Edward Grey; quoted in Callcott (1977: 348).

20 A similar argument is made by John G. Stoessinger (1986) in his *Nations in Darkness*.

6 United States invasions of Grenada and Panama

1 October 25, 1983; American Foreign Policy Current Documents 1983, 1,406.
2 These sentiments were expressed by leaders of other states participating in the invasion. Prime Minister Tom Adams of Barbados, for example, noted that with Bishop's assassination, "Grenada descended into a brutal anarchy, with no government and no institutions other than those maintained by the whim of a gang of murderers" (Institute of Caribbean Studies, 1984:36). Later, both the Reagan Administration and the OECS maintained that there was one legitimate governmental representative in Grenada, the Governor-General of Grenada, Sir Paul Scoon and that Scoon had invited the OECS's military action in Grenada. Arguing the Scoon was a legitimate governmental representative does not contradict the position that Grenada was in a state of anarchy because Scoon was not able to exercise governmental control on the island. For more details on the legal aspects of the invasion, see Davidson, 1987.
3 This point is made somewhat differently by Prime Minister Edward Seaga of Jamaica. He states, "As Caribbean brothers willing and able to assist each other, we must now ensure that the future can be one of solid cooperation in which Grenada will no longer be the odd man out, but be once again welcomed into the family of Caribbean nations" (Institute of Caribbean Studies, 1984:73).
4 Article 8, Number 4 of the Treaty Establishing the Organization of Eastern Caribbean States notes: "The Defense and Security Community shall have responsibility for coordinating the efforts of Member States for collective defense and the preservation of peace and security against external aggression ..."
5 Transcript of a Press Conference by President Reagan, November 3, 1983.
6 Elsewhere, I have analyzed the "sexual abuse" of the Panama invasion through the work of Luce Irigaray, a poststructuralist psychoanalyst. A symptomatic reading of the discourse on the US invasion of Panama suggests that both George Bush and Manuel Noriega are hysterical males competing for access to a feminine object, the Panama Canal. See Weber (1994).
7 All other regional and international organizations which commented on the US lead multinational military operation in Grenada condemned it as a violation of the sovereignty of Grenada and described it as an act of intervention.
8 This point is highly contested. For a discussion of Scoon's supposed legal authority, see Shahabuddeen, 1986: chapter 5 and Davidson, 1987: chapter 4).
9 The invasion discourse slips back even further to a dress rehearsal of the invasion in 1981. According to the war-game script of "Operation Ocean Venture '81," US Army Rangers invade an Eastern Caribbean island called "Amber and the Amberdines" in order to free American hostages and establish a government that is friendly toward the US. "Amber and the Amberdines" was "widely understood as referring to Grenada and its two dependencies, the Grenadines" (Barry et al., 1984:321).

136

10 One might suggest that because the Panama invasion is a matter of US domestic policy rather than foreign policy, the Bush Administration may serve as the community of judgment about the Panamanian election. Although this is problematic (because the election proceeded the invasion by several months), this move does not escape a logic of simulation because the Bush Administration must trace its support back to the American people, who are simulated. The American people appear in Bush Administration invasion discourse as results of public opinion surveys.

7 Symbolic exchange and state

1 Baudrillard (1990:74).
2 For an account of sovereignty and United Nations membership in an order of simulation, see Timothy Luke (1993).

REFERENCES

Albrecht-Carrie, René, ed. (1968) *The Concert of Europe*. London: Macmillan.

Albrecht-Carrie, René (1970) *Britain and France: Adaptations to a Changing Context of Power*. Garden City, New York: Doubleday.

Albrecht-Carrie, René (1973) *A Diplomatic History of Europe Since the Congress of Vienna*. New York: Harper & Row.

American Foreign Policy Current Documents (various years) Washington, DC: US Government Printing Office.

Ashley, Richard K. (1989a) Living on Border Lines: Man, Poststructuralism, and War. In *International/ Intertextual Relations*, edited by J. Der Derian and M. J. Shapiro, pp. 259–321. Lexington, MA: Lexington Books.

Ashley, Richard K. (1989b) Untying the Sovereign State: A Double Reading of the Anarchy Problematique. *Millennium: Journal of International Studies* 17:227–62.

Baker, R. S. (1927–1939) *Woodrow Wilson: Life and Letters*. Garden City, NJ: Doubleday, Page & Co.

Baker, R. S. and W. E. Dodd, eds. (1925–1927) *The Public Papers of Woodrow Wilson*. New York: Harper & Bros.

Barry, Tom, Beth Wood, and Deb Preusch (1984) *The Other Side of Paradise: Foreign Control in the Caribbean*. New York: Grove Press.

Baudrillard, Jean (1983a) *Simulations*, translated by P. Foss, P. Patton, and P. Beitchman. New York: Semiotext(e).

Baudrillard, Jean (1983b) *In the Shadow of the Silent Majorities*, translated by P. Foss, J. Johnston, and P. Patton. New York: Semiotext(e).

Baudrillard, Jean (1987a) *Forget Foucault*. New York: Semiotext(e).

Baudrillard, Jean (1987b) *The Ecstasy of Communication*, translated by B. and C. Schutze; edited by S. Lotringer. New York: Semiotext(e).

Baudrillard, Jean (1988) Symbolic Exchange and Death, pp. 119–48. In: *Jean Baudrillard: Selected Writings*, edited and introduced by Mark Poster. Stanford: Stanford University Press.

Baudrillard, Jean (1990) *Seduction*, translated by B. Singer. New York: St. Martin's Press.

Baudrillard, Jean (1992) Transpolitics, Transsexuality, Transaesthetics, pp. 9–26. In: *Jean Baudrillard: The Disappearance of Art and Politics*, edited by William Stearns and William Chaloupka. New York: St. Martin's.

Beik, P. H., ed. (1970) *The French Revolution*. New York: Walker and Company.

Biersteker, Thomas, Janice E. Thomson, and Cynthia Weber (1993) State Sovereignty as Social Construct: Toward a New Research Agenda. Unpublished manuscript.

Bradlee, Ben Jr. (1988) *Guts and Glory: The Rise and Fall of Oliver North.* New York: Donald I. Fine, Inc.

British Foreign and State Papers (various years) London: HM Stationery Office.

Bull, Hedley, ed. (1984) *Intervention in World Politics.* Oxford: Oxford University Press.

Callcott, W. H. (1977) *The Caribbean Policy of the United States, 1890–1920.* New York: Octagon Books.

Campbell, David (1992) *Writing Security: United States Foreign Policy and the Politics of Identity.* Minneapolis: University of Minnesota Press.

Caporaso, James A., ed. (1989) *The Elusive State: International and Coomparative Perspectives.* Newbury Park: Sage.

Carnoy, Martin (1984) *The State and Political Theory.* Princeton, NJ: Princeton University Press.

Carr, R. (1966) *Spain, 1808–1939.* Oxford: Clarendon Press.

Committee on Armed Services (1990) *1989 Events in Panama.* Joint Hearings before the Committee on Armed Services and the Select Committee on Intelligence, US Senate, October 6 and 17; December 22, 1989. S. Hrg. 101–881. Washington: US Government Printing Office.

Connolly, William (1987) *Politics and Ambiguity.* Madison: University of Wisconsin Press.

Connolly, William (1993) Democracy and Territoriality. In *Rhetorical Republic: Governing Representations in American Politics,* edited by Frederick M. Dolan and Thomas L. Dumm. Amherst, MA: University of Massachusetts Press.

Culler, Jonathan (1982) *On Deconstruction: Theory and Criticism after Structuralism.* Ithaca, NY: Cornell University Press.

Current Policy (various years) Washington, DC: US Department of State.

Davidson, Scott (1987) *Grenada: A Study in Politics and the Limits of International Law.* Aldershot, England: Avebury.

Doty, Roxanne (1993) Sovereignty and National Identity: Constructing the Nation. Unpublished Manuscript.

Dreyfus, H. L. and P. Rabinow (1982) *Michel Foucault: Beyond Structuralism and Hermeneutics.* Chicago: University of Chicago Press.

Duner, B. (1985) *Military Intervention in Civil Wars: The 1970s.* NY: St. Martin's Press.

Evans, Peter et al. (1985) *Bringing the State Back In.* Cambridge: Cambridge University Press.

Falk, Richard (1963) *Law, Morality and War in the Contemporary World.* London: Pall Mall.

Fischer, Markus (1992) Feudal Europe, 800–1300: Communal Discourse and Conflictual Practices. *International Organization* 46(2):427–66.

Foreign Relations of the United States (various years) Washington, DC: United States Government Printing Office.

Foreign Relations of the United States, 1914–1920, Lansing Papers (1939) vol. 2, Washington DC: United States Government Printing Office.

Foreign Relations of the United States, 1918–1919, Russia (1931–1937) vol. 2, Washington, DC: United States Government Printing Office.

Foucault, Michael (1979) *Discipline and Punish: The Birth of the Prison*, translated by A. Sheridan. New York: Vintage Books.

Foucault, Michael (1980a) "Two Lectures," In: *Power/Knowledge: Selected Interviews and Other Writings 1972–1977*, edited by Colin Gorden and trans. by Colin Gorden et al. New York: Pantheon Books.

Foucault, Michael (1980b) *The History of Sexuality, Volume 1: An Introduction*, translated by Robert Hurley. New York: Vintage.

Gain, Mark (1991a) *Baudrillard: Critical and Fatal Theory*. New York: Routledge.

Gain, Mark (1991b) *Baudrillard's Bestiary: Baudrillard and Culture*. New York: Routledge.

Gardner, Lloyd C. (1976) *Wilson and Revolutions: 1913–1921*. Philadelphia: J. B. Lippincott.

Gardner, Lloyd C. (1982) Woodrow Wilson and the Mexican Revolution. In: *Woodrow Wilson and a Revolutionary World, 1913–1921*, edited by A. S. Link, pp. 3–48. Chapel Hill: University of North Carolina Press.

Geertz, Clifford (1973) *The Interpretation of Cultures*. New York, NY: Basic Books.

Greene, T. P. (1957) *Wilson at Versailles*. Boston: Heath.

Grieco, Joseph M. (1988) Anarchy and the Limits of Cooperation: A Realist Critique of the Newest Liberal Institutionalism. *International Organization* 42(3):485–507.

Gurr, Ted, ed.(1980) *Handbook of Political Conflict: Theory and Research*. New York, NY: Free Press

Gurr, Ted (1988) War, Revolution and Growth of the Coercive State. *Comparative Political Studies* 21:45–65.

Hall, J. A. and G. J. Ikenberry (1989) *The State*. Minneapolis: University of Minnesota Press.

Hart, John M. (1987) *Revolutionary Mexico: The Coming and Process of the Mexican Revolution*. Berkeley: University of California Press.

Haas, Ernst (1969) "Letter to the Editor" *Journal of Common Market Studies* 8:70.

Held, David (1989) *Political Theory and the Modern State: Essays on State, Power, and Democracy*. Stanford: Stanford University Press.

Herz, John (1957) Rise and Demise of the Territorial State. *World Politics* 9:473–93.

Herz, John (1969) The Territorial State Revisited: Reflections on the future of the nation-state. In: *International Politics and Foreign Policy: A Reader in Research and Theory*, edited by J. N. Rosenau, pp. 76–89. New York: The Free Press.

Higgins, R. (1984) Intervention and International Law. In: *Intervention in World Politics*, edited by H. Bull, pp. 29–44. Oxford: Oxford University Press.

Hinsley, F. H. (1986) *Sovereignty*, 2nd edn. Cambridge: Cambridge University Press.

Hoffmann, Stanley (1984) The Problem of Intervention. In: *Intervention in World Politics*, edited by H. Bull, pp. 7–28. Oxford: Oxford University Press.

Inayatullah, Naeem (1993) Beyond the Sovereignty Dilemma: International Society, Global Division of Labor and Third World States. Unpublished manuscript.

Institute of Caribbean Studies (1984) *Documents on the Invasion of Grenada,*

Supplement No. 1 to *Caribbean Monthly Bulletin*, October, 1983. Rio Piedras, Puerto Rico: University of Puerto Rico.

Jackson, Robert H. (1990) *Quasi-States: Sovereignty, International Relations, and the Third World*. Cambridge: Cambridge University Press.

James, Alan (1986) *Sovereign Statehood: The Basis of International Society*. London: Allen & Unwin.

Jennings, W. I. (1965) *The Approach of Self Government*. Cambridge: Cambridge University Press.

Johnston, R. J. (1986) Placing Politics: Colston Society Guest Lecture, 3 April 1986. *Political Geography Quarterly* 5(4):563–78.

Kegley, Charles W., Jr. (1993) The Neoidealist Movement in International Studies? Realist Myths and the New International Realities. *International Studies Quarterly* 37(2):131–46.

Keohane, Robert O. (1984) *After Hegemony: Cooperation and Discord in the World Political Economy*. Princeton: Princeton University Press.

Keohane, Robert O. and Joseph S. Nye (1977) *Power and Interdependence: World Politics in Transition*. Boston: Little, Brown.

Kissinger, Henry A. (1964) *A World Restored: Metternich, Castlereagh and the Problems of Peace, 1812–22*. Boston: Houghton Mifflin.

Krasner, Stephen D. (1983) Structural Causes and Regime Consequences: Regimes as Intervening Variables, pp. 1–22. In: *International Regimes*, edited by Stephen D. Krasner. Ithaca: Cornell University Press.

Larson, Deborah Welch (1985) *Origins of Containment: A Psychological Explanation*. Princeton: Princeton University Press.

Lefebvre, G. (1947) *The Coming of the French Revolution*, translated by R. R. Palmer. Princeton, NJ: Princeton University Press.

Levin, N. Gordon, Jr. (1968) *Woodrow Wilson and World Politics: America's Response to War and Revolution*. New York: Oxford University Press.

Link, Arthur S. (1954) *Woodrow Wilson and the Progressive Era 1910–1917*. New York: Harper & Brothers Pub.

Link, Arthur S. (1979) *Woodrow Wilson: Revolution, War, and Peace*. Arlington Heights, IL: Harlan Davidson, Inc.

Little, Richard (1975) *Intervention: External Involvement in Civil Wars*. Totowa, NJ: Rowman and Littlefield.

Little, Richard (1987) Revisiting Intervention: A Survey of Recent Developments. *Review of International Studies* 13:49–60.

Luke, Timothy (1989) *Screens of Power: Ideology, Domination, and Resistance in Informational Scoeity*. Urbana: University of Illinois Press.

Luke, Timothy (1991) The Discipline of Security Studies and the Codes of Containment: Learning From Kuwait. *Alternatives* 16:315–44.

Luke, Timothy W. (1993) Discourses of Disintegration, Texts of Transformation: Re-Reading Realism in the New World Order. *Alternatives* 18(2):229–58.

Metternich, C. (1970) *Memoirs of Prince Metternich, 1815–1829*, vols. 3 and 4. Edited by Prince R. Metternich. Translated by Napier. New York: Howard Fertig.

Mitchell, C. R. (1970) Civil Strife and the Involvement of External Parties. *International Studies Quarterly* 14:166–94.

Morgan, Edmund S. (1988) *Inventing the People: The Rise of Popular Sovereignty in England and America*. New York: W.W. Norton & Company.

Murphy, Alexander (1990) Historical Justifications for Territorial Claims. *Annals of the Association of American Geographers* 80(4):531–48.

New York Times (1914), April 24.

Onuf, Nicholas Greenwood (1991) Sovereignty: Outline of a Conceptual History. *Alternatives* 16(4):425–46.

Palmer, R. R. and J. Colton (1971) *A History of the Modern World*, 4th edn. New York: Alfred A. Knopf.

Pearson, Fredrick (1974) Foreign Military Interventions and Domestic Disputes. *International Studies Quarterly* 18:259–89.

Poggi, Gianfranco (1978) *The Development of the Modern State: A Sociological Introduction*. Stanford: Stanford University Press.

Public Papers of the President: George Bush 1989, vol. 2 (1990) Washington, DC: US Government Printing Office.

Public Papers of the President: George Bush 1990, vol. 1 (1991) Washington, DC: US Government Printing Office.

Public Papers of the President: Ronald Reagan, 1983, vol. 2 (1985) Washington, DC: US Government Printing Office.

Raymond, G. A. and Charles Kegley (1987) Normative Constraints on the Use of Force Short of War. *Journal of Peace Research* 23:213–27.

Robinson, E. E. and V. J. West (1917) *The Foreign Policy of Woodrow Wilson, 1913–1917*. New York: Macmillan.

Rosecrance, Richard N. (1963) *Action and Reaction in World Politics: International Systems in Perspective*. Boston: Little and Brown.

Rosenau, James (1968) The Concept of Intervention. *Journal of International Affairs* 22:165–76.

Rosenau, James (1969) Intervention as a Scientific Concept. *Journal of Conflict Resolution* 13:149–71.

Ruggie, John G. (1983) Continuity and Transformation in the World Polity: Toward a Neorealist synthesis. *World Politics* 35:261–85.

Ruggie, John G. (1989) International Structure and International Transformation: Space, Time, and Method. In: *Global Change and Theoretical Challenge: Approaches to World Politics in the 1990s*, edited by E-O. Czempiel and J. N. Rosenau, pp. 21–35. Lexington, MA: Lexington Books.

Ruggie, John Gerard (1993) Territoriality and Beyond: Problematizing Modernity in International Relations. *International Organization* 47(1):139–74.

Ryle, G. (1949) *The Concept of Mind*. New York: Barnes & Noble.

Sack, R. D. (1981) Territorial Bases of Power. In *Political Studies from Spatial Perspectives*, A. D. Burnett and P. J. Taylor, eds. New York: John Wiley and Sons.

Sack, R. D. (1983) Human Territoriality: A Theory. *Annals of the Association of American Geographers* 73:55–74.

Saussure, Ferdinand de (1974) *Course in General Linquistics*, edited by Tullio de Mauro. London: Fontana.

Schenk, H. G. (1967) *The Aftermath of the Napoleonic Wars: The Concert of Europe – An Experiment*. New York: Howard Fertig.

Schroeder, P. W. (1962) *Metternich's Diplomacy at Its Zenith, 1820–1823*. Austin: University of Texas Press.

Scott, J. B. (1918) *President Wilson's Foreign Policy: Messages, Addresses, Papers.* New York: Oxford University Press.

Shahabuddeen, M. (1986) *The Conquest of Grenada: Sovereignty in the Periphery.* Georgetown, Guyana: University of Guyana Press.

Sikkink, Kathryn (1993) Human Rights, Principled Issue- Networks, and Sovereignty in Latin America. *International Organization* 47(3):411–41.

Singer, J. David and M. Small (1969) National Alliance Committments and War Involvement, 1818–1945. In: *International Politics and Foreign Policy: A Reader in Research and Theory*, edited by J. N. Rosenau, pp. 513–30. New York: The Free Press.

Singer, J. David and M. Small (1972) *The Wages of War 1816–1965: A Statistical Handbook*. New York: John Wiley & Sons, Inc.

Singer, J. David and M. Small (1982) *Resort to Arms: Intervention and Civil Wars 1816–1980*. Beverly Hills, CA: Sage Publications.

Siverson, R. M. and M. R. Tennefoss (1982) Interstate Conflicts: 1815–1965. *International Interactions* 9:147–78.

Skocpol, Theda (1985) Bringing the State Back In: Strategies of Analysis in Current Research. In *Bringing the State Back In*, edited by P. B. Evans, D. Rueschemeyer, and T. Skocpol. Cambridge: Cambridge University Press.

Speakes, Larry with R. Pack (1988) *Speaking Out: Inside the Reagan White House*. New York: Scribners.

Spivak, Gayatri Chakravoty (1976) Translator's Preface. In: *Of Grammatology* by Jacques Derrida, trans. by G. Spivak, Baltimore: The Johns Hopkins University Press, pp. ix-xc.

Stoessinger, John G. (1986) *Nations in Darkness: China, Russia, and America*, 4th edn. New York: Random House.

Temperley, H. (1966) *The Foreign Policy of Canning, 1822–1827: England, the Neo-holy Alliance, and the New World*. London: Archon Books.

Thomas, C. (1985) *New States, Sovereignty, and Intervention*. New York: St. Martin's Press.

Thomson, Janice E. (1990) State Practices, International Norms, and the Decline of Mercenarism. *International Studies Quarterly* 34:23–47.

Thomson, Janice E. (1994) *Mercenaries, Pirates, and Sovereignty: State-Building and Extraterritorial Violence in Early Modern Europe*. Princeton: Princeton University Press.

Van Winger, J. and H. Tillema (1980) British Military Intervention after WWII. *Journal of Peace Research* 17:291–303.

Van Winger, J. and H. Tillema (1982) Law and Power in Military Intervention: Major States after World War II. *International Studies Quarterly* 26:220–50.

Vernon, Raymond (1971) *Sovereignty at Bay: The Multinational Spread of US Enterprises*. New York: Basic Books.

Vernon, Raymond (1991) Sovereignty at Bay: Twenty Years After. *Millennium* 20(2):191–5.

Vincent, Richard J. (1974) *Nonintervention and International Order*. Princeton, NJ: Princeton University Press.

143

Walker, R. B. J. (1988) *One World, Many Worlds: Struggles for a Just World Peace.* Boulder, CO: Lynne Reinner Publishers.

Walker, R. B. J. (1990) On the Discourses of Sovereignty: Gender and Critique in the Theory of International Relations (draft). Paper presented at the annual meetings of the International Studies Association, Washington, DC, April.

Walker, R. B. J. (1993) *Inside/Outside: International Relations as Political Theory.* Cambridge: Cambridge University Press.

Weber, Cynthia (1994) Something's Missing: Male Hysteria and the US Invasion of Panama. *Genders* 19: 171–97.

Webster, C. K. (1958) *The Foreign Policy of Castlereagh, 1815–1822.* London: G. Bell and Sons.

Weede, E. (1978) US Support for Foreign Governments or Domestic Disorder and Imperial Intervention 1958–1965. *Comparative Political Studies* 10: 497–527.

Wendt, Alexander E. (1988) The State System and the Structuring of Global Militarization. Paper presented at the 1988 Annual Meeting of the American Political Science Association, Washington, D.C.

Wendt, Alexander E. (1992) Anarchy is What States Make of it: The Social Construction of Power Politics. *International Organization* 46: 391–425.

Wight, Martin (1977) *Systems of States.* Leicester: Leicester University Press.

Wilson, Woodrow (1908) *Constitutional Government in the United States.* New York: Harper and Bros.

144

INDEX

Adams, Tom, 109, 111
Albrecht-Carrie, Rene, 41

Baudrillard, Jean, 31, 34–9, 112, 121, 126
Baudrillardian approach
  alibi function, 128–9
  critique of Foucault, 35–6
  hyperreal, 128
  logic of simulation, 34, 107
  overview, 34–9
  seduction, 38–9, 106, 112, 126
  simulacrum, 37
  simulation, 34, 37–9, 107, 112, 122, 125–9
Bolshevik Revolution, 14, 28, 72, 93, 114
Bolshevism, 76, 77, 86
Bradlee, Ben, 110
Brest-Litovsk Treaty, 74, 75, 76, 78
Bush Administration
  definition of intervention, 106, 119–20
  intervention in Panama, 125, 127, 128
  justifications for intervention in
    Panama, 105
Bush, George, 15

Caricom, 108
Carranza government,
  US recognition of, 66
Carranza, Venustiano, 67
Castlereagh, 42, 43, 54
  British case against collective
    intervention, 47–8, 54, 55–6, 58–60
Charles, Eugenia, 94
Concert of Europe, 13, 22, 24
  British case against collective
    intervention, 47–8, 54, 55–6, 58–60
  collective right of intervention, 44
  doctrine of legitimacy, 43–50, 58–60
  formation of, 42
  interventions as mark, 32–3
  interventions in Spain and Naples, 13,
    33, 124
  justifications for intervention, 44–5
  members, 42
  principles of, 42–5
Congress of Troppau, 49, 50, 56

Circular, 50–1
  Metternich's "Points," 51–2
  Protocol, 52–3, 56

Declaration of the Rights of Man and
  Citizen, 41
domestic/international boundary, 13, 16,
  25
  as truth-effect, 126
  discursive erasure of, 99, 102–6
  effects of domestication of Panama on,
    119–20
  Endara government, 101, 125
  simulation of, 107, 116–18, 125, 127–8

Endara, Guillermo, 116

Falk, Richard, 21
Foucauldian approach
  discipline, 31, 124–5
  mark, 30–1, 34, 39, 54, 123–4
  overview, 31–4
  power to punish, 30, 31
  power/knowledge, 30, 33–4, 35–8, 124–6
  sign, 30–3, 34–5, 61, 123–4
  theory of the object, 37
  trace, 30–1, 32, 34, 39, 107, 123–4
Foucault, Michel, 30, 31–4, 112
French Revolution, 35, 40–1, 44, 73, 80, 85

Gardner, Lloyd, 75
Geertz, Clifford, 21
Grenada
  intervention justification, 15
  Revolutionary Military Council, 111
  simulation of, 112–15, 126–7
  US invasion of, 14, 15, 38, 92–9, 105,
    107–15, 128

Haas, Ernst, 1
Hoffmann, Stanley, 17
Huerta, Victoriano, 12, 62
  government, 62, 63–6

Idealism, 1

145

as location of state, 124
definition, 1–2
effects of domestication of Panama on,
  115–22
erasure of, 120–2
first principle, 20–1
foundations, 7–8
in logic of simulation, 126–9
ontology, 3, 6
sovereignty/intervention boundary,
  11–12, 112
spatial dimension, 2–3
temporal dimension, 2–3
uncontested concept, 2
simulation of, 121–2, 127–9
Spanish Revolution, 48
Speakes, Larry, 109
state
  and symbolic exchange, 123–9
  as sign, 123
  as sovereignty/intervention boundary,
    23–4, 25–6
  as stabilized by sovereignty, 12–15
  in logic of simulation, 127–9

Taft Administration
  policy toward Mexico, 62
thick description, 21–3
thin description, 21–3
Third Estate, 40–1
Treaty of Aix-la-Chapelle
  Tsar Alexander's interpretation of, 53
Trotsky, 76
Tsar Alexander, 53
Tsar Nicholas II, 72, 73, 89
  government, 72

US invasion of Grenada
  as fatal to representation, 127
  as rescue mission, 93,114
  contrast to Soviet invasion of
    Afghanistan, 97–8,113
  justifications for, 93
  legal justifications, 98-9
United Nations, 15, 108

Villa, Francisco "Pancho," 67
  attack on Columbus, New Mexico, 67
Vincent, R.J., 20, 21

Walker, R.B.J., 2, 11
War on Drugs, 13, 16, 92, 104–6, 119,
  120
  combatting drug trafficking, 100, 102–3,
    119–21
  drug trade as intervention, 119–20
Wilson Administration
  definition of intervention, 65–6, 70–1,
    76–7, 81–2
  intervention in Mexico, 35, 61–72, 84–6
  intervention in Siberia, 35, 72–80,
    86–91
  justifications for intervention in
    Mexico, 64–5, 66–7
  justifications for intervention in Siberia,
    79–80
  liberal internationalist agenda, 76
  opposition to Bolshevism, 86, 89, 90
  self-determination, 81–4, 87, 88, 91
Wilson, Woodrow, 12, 14, 22, 28, 61, 115
  Constitutional Government in the United
    States, 85
World War I, 76

147

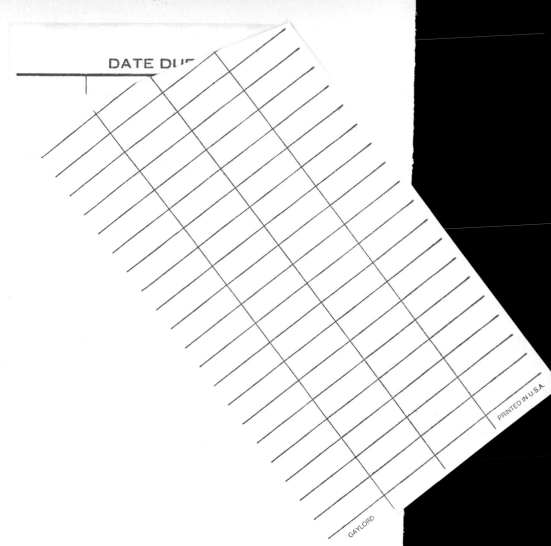

DATE DUE

GAYLORD

PRINTED IN U.S.A.